101 FINISHING TOUCHES
STYLISH HOME IDEAS

Hylas Publishing
Publisher: Sean Moore
Creative Director: Karen Prince
Designer: Gus Yoo
Editor: Beth Adelman

First Published in 2003 by
BBC Worldwide Ltd,
Woodlands, 80 Wood Lane, London W12 0TT
All photographs © BBC *Good Homes* magazine
2003. Please see page 223 for a list of the
contributors.

Published in the United States by
Hylas Publishing
129 Main Street, Irvington,
New York 10533

ISBN 1-59258-026-2

Edited by Alison Willmott
Commissioning Editor: Vivien Bowler
Project Editor: Julia Charles
Series Design: Claire Wood
Book Design: Kathryn Gammon
Design Manager: Annette Peppis
Production Controller: Christopher Tinker

First American Edition published in 2003
02 03 04 05 10 9 8 7 6 5 4 3 2 1

Set in Amasis MT and ITC Officina Sans

Printed and bound in the UK by Butler and
Tanner, Ltd.
Color origination by Radstock Reproductions,
Midsomer Norton

Distributed by St. Martin's Press

101 FINISHING TOUCHES
STYLISH HOME IDEAS

Julie Savill

HYLAS
PUBLISHING

BBC

CONTENTS

INTRODUCTION

How often have you finished decorating a room only to think that it doesn't look quite right, that somehow something is missing? Once the fresh paint is on the walls, the new blinds are on the windows and the furniture is in place, there's still one more step to go before your room makeover is complete. That final stage is to put your individual personality into the room, and it's what this book is about. *101 Finishing Touches* is crammed full of all the little ideas that put the designer's seal on a room, and it's these tiny touches that will bring any decorating scheme to life and make it completely your own.

At *BBC Good Homes* magazine, we believe these little design tricks should be quick to create (an hour is about the most many of us can spare to make something), affordable (why make it if you could buy it ready-made for less?) and full of impact. We have a wealth of clever projects that meet these criteria, and they are all here in *101 Finishing Touches* ready for you to use to add an individual touch to your home. None of them need any specialist skills, and anyone who has an urge to get creative will be able to tackle all of the projects found here.

One word I would add here is to anyone who thinks they can't sew. Do yourself a favor and give it a try. A simple sewing machine is a small investment that will pay for itself time and time again. Even if you only feel confident stitching a straight line it will mean you can make your own cushion covers, blinds, simple curtains and bed spreads, saving you hundreds and hundreds of dollars and giving you access to unlimited looks for your home.

Get into sewing and suddenly the remnant fabric counter at your local department store becomes a treasure chest that you won't be able to pass by. Most department stores have demonstration areas where you can test different sewing machines, ask questions and get advice. Go on, surprise yourself and try it!

Stylists who work on magazines and television make-over programs know all about the importance of the finishing touches, and they have all developed signature tricks of the trade that they keep reinventing and using again and again to draw a scheme together and make it look truly complete. At *BBC Good Homes* magazine we've been lucky enough to work with some of the very best stylists, who are just brimming with ideas for finishing touches. Our special thanks go to Kitty Percy, Alison Jenkins, Juliet Bawden and Petra Boase. I would also like to mention Sophie Robinson, *BBC Good Homes* magazine's talented home editor and her equally skilful predecessor, Wendy Uren, who have both contributed ideas to this book and have also commissioned and overseen the creation of virtually all of the projects here —my thanks to you both.

Julie Savill, Editor
BBC Good Homes magazine

Modern mosaic

The Romans turned them into fine art, but modern mosaics have simpler designs. Follow these steps to make a chic framed mirror. The smaller one is even easier; it uses mirror tiles, which need no grouting.

1 Take a 12 -inch square of 3/4-inch particle board and seal with a mix of half all-purpose white glue, half water. Leave to dry. Using a razor knife, cut borders two tiles wide from sheets of quarter-inch thick dark and pale gray glass mosaic tiles. The outer edges of the larger border should measure 12 1/8 inches, so they overhang the particle board by 1/8 inch. Apply all-purpose white glue to the tiled side of this border, position on the board, then repeat for the inner border. Leave to dry.

2 Cut mosaic strips one tile wide for the mirror edges. Squeeze white glue onto the tiled side and press in place so they line up with the border tiles. Leave until the glue is dry.

3 To remove backing paper, dampen with a sponge and leave for a few minutes. If it does not peel off easily, dampen again. Stick a 5 3/4 × 5 3/4-inch piece of mirror to the particle board using white glue and leave to dry.

4 Mix the white grout following the manufacturer's instructions. Using a rubber squeegee, work it into the mosaic to fill the cracks. Repeat along the sides, remove excess with a damp sponge and leave to dry for two days. Wipe clean using a nylon scrubber and a mild liquid cleaner.

TIP
If, after removing the backing paper, you find that the glue has seeped between the tiles, remove it using the scalpel. Secure any loose tiles using Superglue.

Natural framework

A touch of natural texture adds interest to cool, contemporary interiors, and this seagrass-covered picture frame is smart enough to blend in beautifully. Seagrass varies in color and thickness, so it gives an irregular finish that adds to the natural charm. Choose a frame that has a wide border with a plain, smooth surface.

1 Cut strands of seagrass to fit the borders of your frame. The strands to go along the top and bottom parts of the border should be long enough to pass right across the frame and over the edges, so that their ends are concealed at the back. The strands to cover the vertical sides should be cut to finish level with the top and bottom edges of the picture. Before gluing them down, lay all the strands in place on the frame to check that you have cut enough.

2 Cover the frame with contact adhesive, choosing a glue that remains tacky for awhile before drying. Starting with the vertical strands and working from the inside of the border to the edges, carefully stick each length of seagrass in place. Make sure the ends of the vertical strands line up exactly. Glue down the ends of the horizontal strands at the back of the frame. Leave to dry.

3 To finish, seal your work by brushing the surface of the seagrass with a solution of half all-purpose white glue and half water.

TIP
If you want a slightly different look, try covering a frame with other types of rope or twine, or even bulky knitting wool.

All the best circles

A lively design of squares and circles turns a boring wooden picture frame into an eye-catching contemporary accessory. Cut from paper, the shapes are simply glued in place. The choice of colors is up to you—here soft yellows in closely subtly varying shades complement the mellow honey-colored wood of the frame. It's best to use thin paper, unless you want a slightly raised effect.

1 Take a plain wooden picture frame with a smooth border and measure the sides to work out how wide the strips of paper need to be. Remove the backing from the frame.

2 Using sharp scissors, cut strips of the same width from paper in two or three shades of the same color, making them long enough to wrap around the sides and inner edges of the frame. Glue in place with all-purpose glue and leave to dry.

3 Cut circles in two different sizes from the same paper, drawing around a coin or a bottle top to get the shape. Stick a larger circle of a contrasting shade in the center of some of the squares, including the uncovered wooden ones. When the glue is dry, stick a smaller circle of another shade inside some of the circles.

4 When dry, give the frame a protective finish by covering it with several coats of clear spray varnish, allowing each coat to dry before applying the next.

TIP
If the glue seems thick, thin it by stirring in a small amount of water.

Sea view

Show off a seashore find and a favorite photograph at the same time by turning a piece of rugged driftwood into an unusual picture holder. Driftwood comes in many shapes and sizes, but for this project you will need a reasonably straight piece that isn't too soft. The picture frame is made from two pieces of glass—ask the merchant where you buy the glass to grind the edges so that they are safe to handle.

1 Use a fret saw to cut a quarter-inch slot in a piece of driftwood. To do this, drill a hole, feed the saw blade through, attach it to the saw and then start sawing.

2 Sandwich your photo between the two sheets of glass and push them into the slot. You may need to slip a strip of square dowel into the slot first, to make a ledge for the glass to stand on.

TIP
Before taking items from a beach, check that it is not a special conservation site. Never remove anything from the tide line of debris at the high water mark, which is home to insects and plant life.

Behind the scenes

Clip frames are among the cheapest you can buy, but it takes just seconds to give them an individual look. All you need is a favorite piece of fabric to form a backdrop for your chosen photo. Look for one that will complement the scheme of your room—here a snip of crisp navy and white ticking sits well among the cool blues of a contemporary interior. Fabrics offer a vast choice of designs and colors, but use your imagination and you're bound to come up with many other materials that will also look good. Examples might include textured handmade papers in different colors, tin foil or wallpaper samples.

1 Cut a piece of fabric exactly the same size as the clip frame. Glue your photo in position on the right side of the fabric or, if you like to change your pictures frequently, use poster putty to hold it in place.

2 Take the frame apart, slip the fabric and photo inside, then clip the frame back together—couldn't be simpler!

Shine on

A touch of gold or silver can have a magical effect on uninspiring accessories, transforming them into glamorous features of your room. This mirror frame is embellished with silver gilt cream, which shines against a background of powdery blue. The silver is applied to raised squares, created using a simple relief stenciling technique.

1 Paint a plain wooden mirror frame with a base coat of pale blue water-based paint and leave to dry. To make a stencil, mark evenly spaced squares on a strip of stencil card or acetate (don't use paper, as this will collect moisture and become soggy). Cut out the squares to make a stencil.

2 Place the stencil in position on the frame. Apply white artist's oil or acrylic paint thickly to each of the square cutouts using a metal spatula

or an old credit card. Spoon a dollop of paint onto the edge of the card or spatula, and then pull it over the stencil, making sure that all cut areas are filled. Carefully peel away the stencil, without disturbing the raised surface you've created. Repeat until you have stenciled squares all the way down both vertical sides of the frame.

3 When the paint is dry, rub gilt cream over each of the raised squares using a small round brush or your finger.

Piece plan

A classic-style picture goes totally modern if you hang it in a brand new way, so create a novel wall decoration by pulling your print to pieces and mounting each section on a separate foamboard block.

If you don't have a print big enough, you can get a smaller one enlarged at a photocopy shop. You can also ask the shop to customize your image—this one, originally in black and white, has been photocopied in a sepia tone.

1 Using a fine pencil, divide your print into equal squares. Decide on the size of the finished picture and work out how large each square needs to be. Take the print to a photocopy shop and ask them to enlarge each of the squares to the required size. Have the squares laminated—photocopy shops often offer this service.

2 Cut the laminated squares to size, then cut pieces of foamboard to match. Mount the laminated squares on the blocks by gluing them securely in place. Make light pencil marks on the wall to show where each block should be positioned, measuring carefully to space them evenly and ensure that the lines are straight. Attach them to the wall using sticky foam pads or adhesive Velcro.

Bar code art

Everyday images can look quite dramatic when enlarged, and these quirky bar code pictures make bold decorations for a blank wall. They are created by enlarging a standard bar code on a photocopier, then using the result to make a stencil. Because cutting out the lines and numbers for the stencil may take some time, why not use it more than once? Producing a series of identical pictures in different colors and hanging them together will double the impact.

1 Cut a bar code off an empty package and enlarge it on a photocopier, or ask a copy shop to do this for you. Apply a thin mist of spray adhesive to the copy and stick it to stencil material. Some stencil materials can be cut out using a heat pen, which makes the process quicker, but if you don't want to buy a heat pen use stencil card and do the cutting with a craft knife. Before you start, tape the stencil to a wooden board so that you don't damage your work surface. Cut carefully around each of the lines and numbers.

2 Mix gouache or stencil paint to a thick, creamy consistency. Fix the stencil to a stretched canvas using masking tape and apply the paint with a stencil brush, using a quick dabbing motion. Wash the stencil and brush before going on to your next color.

Etched effect

Who would guess that this designer-style decoration for a mirror has been created using a spray can? The intricate art of etching, or rather something that looks convincingly like it, can be achieved in minutes using a can of etching spray, which is available from home improvement stores and craft shops. With the center of the mirror masked off, and flower and leaf shapes pasted onto the rest, the spray reaches only the parts you want it to, resulting in this elegant border.

1 Take a plain mirror with a beveled edge and decide how wide you want the border to be. To mask off the central area, cut a sheet of paper to cover it and stick in position on the glass using spray adhesive. Cover the beveled edges using masking tape.

2 Cut leaf and flower shapes from paper and stick them to the border in a random pattern, again using spray adhesive.

3 Lay the mirror on newspaper. Apply a thin coat of etching spray and leave to dry, then repeat. When the second coat is dry, carefully remove the masking tape and paper shapes.

Bed of roses

A small picture set against a beautiful backing often looks more stunning than an image that fills the entire frame. Rose petals make a fitting backing for this tiny flower picture, adding an air of luxury and rich color to its display in a simple wooden frame. Fresh petals have a strong color but only a short shelf life. If you want a display that will last, press the petals between sheets of blotting paper sandwiched between heavy books for one to three weeks.

1 If you are using fresh petals, press them for an hour or two between wax paper to flatten them. Cut a piece of card the same size as your picture frame and cover with spray adhesive. Arrange the petals on the card, overlapping them to avoid gaps.

2 Spray a little adhesive onto the back of a small photograph or picture. Position it in the center of the petals and press in place. Insert the card into the frame.

Mat finish

Creativity isn't only about being a skilled artist or craftsman; it can also mean using items in new and exciting ways. Look around your home and you'll probably find lots of things that can be grouped together on a wall to make a novel display. Plastic placemats with great photographic images are far too eye-catching to do no more than protect your table, so use some to brighten up a dull corner. Printed mousepads offer a similar ready-to-go art solution.

1 Choosing designs that will complement the color of your wall, gather together a collection of plastic placemats and coasters. Lay them out on the floor first to decide how you want to arrange them.

2 When you have an arrangement you are happy with, fix each mat to the wall using poster strips, available from stationery stores.

TIP
You could also try the group treatment with plates, decorative ceramic tiles, postcards or fancy picture frames.

Snap happy

Slot your holiday snapshots or family photos into this homemade album, which opens out like an accordion to create an instant photo gallery along a shelf or mantelpiece. Easy to make from cardboard, with patterned paper or fabric to brighten up the covers, it also makes a great gift.

1 Cut a strip of cardboard 2 inches wider than your photos and long enough to accommodate as many photos as you want, allowing a 1-inch border around each one. Fold the card like an accordion to make a separate page for each picture.

2 To make decorative front and back covers, cut two pieces of card about 1/8 inch larger all around than the ends of the folds. Cover the front and back covers in patterned paper or fabric. Cut the paper or fabric about 1/4 inch larger all around than the card and glue in place, then fold the edges over to the wrong side and miter them neatly at the corners before sticking in place.

3 Glue the covers to the end pages of the album, trapping lengths of narrow ribbon in between to act as a tie. Fix your pictures in place with stick-on photo corners.

Down memory lane

If your hoard of memorabilia is out of control, it's time to invest in some businesslike boxes and files. Brown cardboard is cheap, functional and just waiting for that personal touch, so pull out a few of your mementos and use them to customize plain containers. Favorite postcards, stamps and even old letters can all be stuck on like a collage.

1 Collect pictures, stamps or any other suitable materials and decide how you want to arrange them on the box. Lay them in place and make light pencil marks on the box at the corners of each item to use as a guide when gluing.

2 Remove the items and apply all-purpose white glue to the back of each one using an artist's brush. Stick them onto the box using the pencil marks as a guide. Wipe away any excess glue immediately (although because white glue dries clear, small amounts shouldn't show). Leave to dry for approximately 10 minutes.

3 Label the boxes with the names of their contents using Letraset, tracing over the letters with a pencil to transfer them to the box. Carefully erase any obvious pencil marks. Finally, pour a little clear, quick-drying acrylic varnish into a dish and paint over your design. For greater protection, apply one or more coats to the entire surface of the box. Leave to dry.

TIP

Try sticking on items that relate to the contents of each container, such as pressed leaves for a box of gardening paraphernalia or a family photo to decorate one full of sentimental snapshots.

In the bag

Too many boxes and bags? Soften up on storage by hiding clutter away in a big laundry bag. Choose a fabric that matches the colors of your room and it will look great hanging from a hook in your bedroom or bathroom. If you want to use the same instructions to make a gift bag, simply use smaller pieces of fabric.

1 Cut front and back panels measuring 25 × 20 inches, one casing of 3 × 50 inches and two ties measuring 2 × 65 inches. Place the front and back panels right sides together and stitch 1/2 inch from the sides and bottom edge, leaving a 1 1/2-inch gap on each side, 4 1/2 inches from the top. Trim seams at corners and turn to right side.

2 Turn under a double 1/4-inch hem around the top edge of the bag and stitch. Sew the short ends of the casing together to form a circle, then press under 1/2 inch along both raw edges. Place the casing inside the bag, with wrong sides facing, so that it covers the 1 1/2 inch gap. Pin and stitch to the bag close to the pressed edges of the casing.

3 Press under 1/4 inch along both long edges of each tie with an iron, then fold in half lengthwise with wrong sides facing and stitch the pressed edges together. Turn in the short raw ends of the ties and hand sew. Thread ties into slots at sides of bag and through casings. Knot tie ends together to make the drawstring.

TIP
If you want to save time, use colorful nylon cord or fabric ribbon for the drawstring instead of making one from scratch.

Shelf improvement

Take a cheap shelf unit and transform it into an eye-catching storage system for kitchenware. A coat of paint turns rough-looking wood slick white, and hooks for mugs and rails for utensils help maximize storage potential.

1 Prepare a wooden unit for painting by filling any holes, then applying primer. Leave to dry, then sand smooth. Apply one or two coats of white gloss paint, letting dry between each coat.

2 Use a handsaw to cut dowels to fit under the top shelf, across the width of the unit. In a well-ventilated space, spray silver paint onto the dowels and a wire hanging shelf unit, and leave to dry. Screw two large cup hooks under the top shelf, 1/4 inch in from the edge on each side. Secure the dowels between the hooks as a utensil rail. Slot the basket over the third shelf.

3 Mark positions for more cup hooks on the underside of one shelf. Use an awl to make a small hole at each mark, then screw them in.

4 Measure the space between the bottom two shelves. Add 3/4 inch to the height and 6 inches to the width and cut a piece of vinyl fabric to this size. Fold in 3/4 inch along one long edge, stick down and attach eyelets, spaced 4 inches apart. Thread the fabric onto a spring-loaded curtain rod, then fix under the bottom shelf.

TIP
Use a piece of colorful plastic shower curtain to cover the bottom shelf. Holes for the curtain rod will already be there.

Retro cut

Give a simple shelf unit a retro look with a pair of oval cut-outs. The shelf and brackets are easy to make from particle board and the ovals can be cut out using a jigsaw. A bright coat of paint completes the look, to create a unit that makes an eye-catching display item in its own right.

1 Draw an oval shape on cardboard and cut around it to make a template. Cut two squares of 3/4-inch thick particle board. Place the template on each particle board square so that its length runs from corner to corner, and draw around it. Wearing a mask, cut out the shape using a jigsaw.

2 Cut a panel of particle board for the top of the shelf. Paint the shelf and brackets in the color and finish (matte, semigloss or glossy) of your choice. Leave to dry.

3 Secure the brackets to the wall, then place the shelf across the top and glue in place using an all-purpose white glue.

File fiesta

Make your home office a more cheerful place to work and every day will seem like a holiday. Start with a line-up of colorful magazine files; sturdy wooden ones are ideal for tidying up papers and books. Slapping on a coat of paint would be the quickest way to jazz them up, but these are colored using a mixture of dye and denatured alcohol. This produces a less opaque finish than regular paint would give, and allows the grain of the wood to show through.

1 Rub down the wood with fine sandpaper to remove any glue residues or varnish. Wearing rubber gloves, pierce a container of cold water dye, pour the contents into a glass measuring cup and add 8 oz of warm water. Dissolve the dye in the water, then add 8 oz of denatured alcohol and stir well.

2 Paint the color onto the magazine files using a small paintbrush or sponge. Add more coats if you want a greater intensity of color. Place the files on paper towels and allow them to dry thoroughly. Finish by applying a coat of protective varnish.

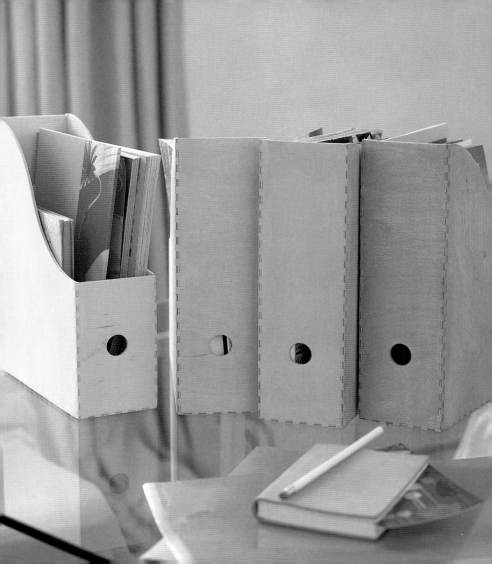

Box room

Old shoe boxes make handy containers for all kinds of things. Covering them with fabric means you can keep them on display rather than hiding them away in a closet. The fabric that transforms this box has been tie-dyed, and the lid is padded to give a soft finish.

1 Wash and iron a length of white, unfinished cotton, then weigh it to find out how much cold water dye you need. To form the pattern shown here, fold the fabric like a paper fan and tie it firmly with thread at 1 1/2-inch intervals. To dye the fabric, follow the instructions for steps 3 and 4 of the tie-dyed tablecloth project on page 82.

2 When the dyed fabric is dry, cut a panel long enough to go around all four sides of the box, allowing about 2 inches extra in the width to turn the fabric in at the top and bottom edges. Cover the box with spray adhesive and stick the fabric in place, gluing the extra fabric at the top to the inside of the box and the extra at the bottom bottom to the base.

3 Cut a piece of padding the same size as the lid and glue it in place on top. Cut fabric to cover the lid and padding, again allowing extra to turn in. Stick the fabric in place on one long side of the lid, then pull it taut over the padding and glue the opposite side. Repeat for the two shorter sides, folding the fabric in neatly at the corners.

Magnetic attraction

Add a metal strip along the front edge of a shelf, and you can use magnets to make it double up as a bulletin board. Gather a selection of stylish refrigerator magnets (skip the cartoon characters) to hold reminders and postcards on the metal surface. As well as being a practical idea, this also provides a stylish finishing touch for a standard shelf. Here shiny stainless steel gives this simple, contemporary design a particularly sleek look.

1 Buy a strip of stainless steel that matches the thickness of the shelf, and cut away any excess length. If you buy it from a sheet metal shop or a home improvement store, they may be able to cut it to size for you.

2 Squeeze a strong adhesive all along the edge of the shelf, or use sturdy double-sided tape. Press the stainless steel strip firmly in place and wipe away any excess glue. If necessary, use tape to keep the strip in position while the glue is drying.

Get stuck in

Découpage is the art of decorating surfaces with paper cutouts, and all it requires is an eye for combining shapes and colors, plus a little careful cutting and pasting. Anyone can create a masterpiece such as this box, which is covered with handmade paper and flower motifs cut from gift wrap. Just make sure you have the right scissors for the job: small, sharp ones such as manicure scissors are essential for tackling the intricate outlines of the flower motifs, while deckle-edged scissors give the mauve stripes their rough-looking edges. A flat brush is also useful, to help you get an even spread of glue.

TIP
Plain wooden accessories and unfinished furniture designed for home painting or decorating are available from mail order suppliers—see Where to Buy on page 210 for details.

1 Using paper glue, cover a wooden box and lid with natural-colored handmade paper, overlapping it at the edges. Trim the edges with a craft knife. Cover the lid edges with strips of mauve handmade paper. Cut narrow strips of mauve paper using deckle-edged scissors and arrange them on the box and lid in a lattice design. Fix securely in place using paper glue.

2 Using sharp manicure scissors, carefully cut flower motifs from gift wrap and stick them to the box, one by one. Brush glue onto the box, press a flower in place and smooth from the center to the edges to remove air bubbles. Wipe off any excess glue with a damp sponge.

3 When the glue is dry, seal the whole box with two coats of clear acrylic varnish, sanding lightly after each coat.

Under cover

Don't throw out those old telephone books when the new ones arrive on your doorstep. Recycle their pages by using them to cover plain boxes, then stack a set together for smart storage. The paper is torn into strips and applied with wallpaper paste using papier-mâché techniques, which means you can use the standard directory pages to cover boxes of any size. If you would prefer your covering to be a little more colorful, try using gift wrap or pages torn from old books or magazines. Look for sturdy cardboard or wooden boxes.

1 Cover your work surface with newspaper, then prepare some wallpaper paste following the manufacturer's instructions.

2 Tear up strips of paper and coat each one with paste by dipping it in, then running it through your fingers to remove any excess. Smooth the strips one by one onto the boxes and lids, overlapping the edges, until they are covered with paper. Leave to dry.

TIP
If you make up too much wallpaper paste, any excess can be stored in a jar with a screw top until you need it again.

Glad hatters

Even if you don't have hats to keep in them, hat boxes make great storage solutions. Big enough to gobble up out-of-season clothes or extra bed linen, their attractive shapes mean you can leave them perched on top of a wardrobe or in the corner of a bedroom without feeling that they spoil the view. Decorative hat boxes can be wildly expensive to buy, but plain cardboard ones are cheaper and easy to decorate. A pretty rose stamp and pink ribbon handles give these plain white boxes a lift, and a larger version of the same stamp is repeated on the wall behind.

1 Buy a small rubber stamp from a home improvement or craft store. Some stamp manufacturers sell special stamp paint, but you can also use stencil paints. Pour a small amount of paint into a dish or old saucer and use a brush or stamp roller to apply a thin, even coat to the raised surface of the stamp. Carefully press the stamp onto the hatbox, then lift off. Repeat until the box is covered with motifs, spacing them evenly.

2 If you are using two colors with one stamp, it is best to stamp each color separately. For example, stamp all the roses in pink and leave to dry, then stamp the leaves in green, making sure you line up the stamp properly with the first part of the motif.

3 Complete your hatbox makeover by cutting a length of narrow ribbon, threading it through the holes to make a handle, and knotting the ends on the inside.

Neat seat

Add an upholstered lid, padded with foam, and a wooden storage box doubles as a comfy bench. You can buy foam rubber from specialist suppliers (see your local phone book), who will usually cut it to size.

1 Lightly sand the box, apply primer, then paint. Remove lid. Make a paper template of the lid and get foam rubber cut to this size.

2 Lay newspaper on the floor, and cover one side of the foam with a spray adhesive for foam. Position foam, glue side down, on lid and leave to dry. Measure the lid, taking the tape measure down to the wood. Cut medium-weight padding and ticking to these dimensions. Cut the top fabric 3/4 inch larger all around.

3 Place the padding over the foam and cover with the ticking, folding in and tacking the corners neatly. Center the fabric over the ticking and use a

staple gun, or tacks and a hammer, to attach it to the side edges of the lid. Work on opposite sides, keeping the fabric straight and spacing the tacks 4 to 6 inches apart. Check the result, and re-hammer any tacks if necessary.

4 Trim excess fabric even with edge of lid. Position braid to cover raw edges of fabric and align with lowest edges of lid. Hammer tacks in around sides of box lid, catching in braid and main fabric. Where the braid joins, fold in raw edges and butt join it, hiding join with a tack. Refit lid.

TIP
Upholstery materials should be fire-resistant. Check that the foam and fabric you choose comply with current safety regulations.

Drill thrill

Here's your chance to go crazy with a drill! With a variety of bits, you can add pierced and dot designs to furniture and storage boxes. This style of decoration particularly suits painted wood because the even surface shows off the pattern well, so it is a useful way of revamping old furniture or personalizing particle board blanks. In this bathroom, the laundry hamper, medicine cabinet and trash can have all been given the drill treatment, showing just a few of the designs you can achieve.

1 Before tackling furnishings, practice on scrap wood. Work on a stable surface, such as a workbench, clamp the wood down and place another piece of wood under the one you are working on. Hold the drill steady, with the bit at a 90° angle to the wood. Experiment with different drill bits: a hole saw attachment will cut doorknob-sized holes, flat wood bits are for medium holes, and wood drill bits come in dozens of sizes. A single countersink bit will bore cone-shaped indentations in a variety of sizes; the harder you press down, the wider and deeper the hollow.

2 When you have a design in mind, lightly sand the wood of the item to be drilled. Mark out the design on the wood using light pencil marks, then do the drilling. Sand or file around your drilled holes.

3 Apply a coat of primer and leave to dry, then add a top coat of water-based or oil-based paint in the color of your choice. If you use a water-based paint, finish with a coat of clear varnish.

TIP
Keep your practice boards and label the holes with the drill bit sizes in case you want to repeat the same design in the future.

Waxing lyrical

Batik works on the principle of resist dyeing: Warm wax is used to draw a design on fabric, which is then dyed. Waxed areas resist the dye, so that when the wax is removed the pattern remains. The pattern here is taken from a body art transfer kit, but you can use any design you like.

1 Following the manufacturer's instructions and wearing rubber gloves, mix orange cold water dye with fixative and salt. Add water to cover a length of white cotton. Wash the fabric, and submerge in the dye while still wet. Leave for an hour, agitating regularly, then remove and rinse until the water runs clear. Leave to dry, then iron.

2 Center the fabric flat over your design. Heat batik wax in a small saucepan, placed over a larger one of simmering water. Using a tool called a tjanting or a very fine paintbrush, trace over the design through the fabric with the wax. When the wax has hardened, dye the fabric red, as in step 1. Leave to dry.

3 Place the fabric between sheets of paper towels and

press with a very hot iron. The wax will melt onto the paper. Repeat with clean paper towels until no more wax is absorbed. Wash and iron the fabric. Cut it to fit your cushion pad, adding a 1/2-inch seam allowance. Stitch three sides, insert pad and slip stitch closed. Make a second cover from a sheer fabric such as rayon, 2 inches larger all around.

TIP
After drawing your design, check the underside of the fabric to make sure the wax has been absorbed right through and is not just sitting on the surface.

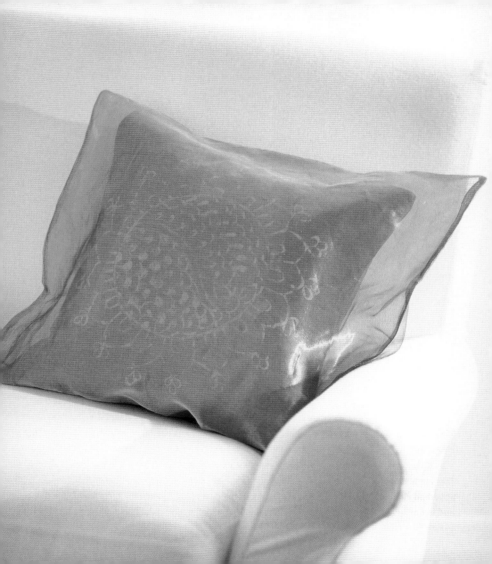

Table topper

If an ugly or shabby table is letting your decor down and you can't afford to replace it, do a hide-and-disguise job by making a simple fabric cover. Loose furniture covers not only conceal a multitude of sins but can also be a quick and easy way of adding a splash of brightness to an otherwise neutral color scheme. For a room with solid furniture, choose heavy wool, brocade or damask, but go for pretty chintz and lighter fabrics for a bright, airy look.

1 Measure your tabletop and add 1 inch to the length and width. Cut the top of your cover to these measurements. Cut four skirt pieces—the ones shown here are 11 inches long, including 1 1/4 inches for seams. Two pieces should be the same length as the top of the cover and two the same width. Sew the skirt pieces together along their short sides, leaving 1/2 inch open at the tops of the seams. Press the seams open.

2 Stitch a 1/4-inch double hem around the lower edge of the skirt. Pin and stitch the skirt to the cover with right sides facing and raw edges matching. Make sure that each seam of the skirt lines up with a corner of the cover.

3 Stitch the skirt to the cover, allowing the top of the skirt seams to open as you go around each corner. Trim off the corners diagonally to reduce bulk, taking care not to cut the stitching. Press seams down toward the skirt. Turn right side out and place over your table.

TIP
Make sure the fabric you choose for a table cover is washable. Alternatively, lay a piece of glass over the top, cut to fit by a glazier.

Cushy numbers

Mounds of cushions piled on a sofa, armchair or bed give a room an inviting feel. If you know how to make a basic cushion cover, it's easy to adapt the design to create any number of individual looks. For example, you could choose fabrics of different colors for the front and back, to provide a stunning contrast. Or you could have the opening at the front and fasten it with decorative buttons, eyelets or ties. Follow the instructions below to make a simple envelope-style cover for a rectangular pillow.

1 Cut one front panel the size of the cushion pad, adding 1 inch to the length and width for seam allowances. Cut one back panel the same size, plus 6 inches for the overlap of the envelope.

2 Fold the back panel in half widthwise, then cut it along the fold into two identical pieces. Stitch a 1/4-inch double hem on both these cut edges.

3 Place the back panels and front panel together, with right sides facing and raw edges matching, so that the back panels overlap by 4 1/4 inches at the center. Stitch a 1/2-inch seam around the outer edges. Trim the seams at the corners to reduce bulk, then turn the cover right side out and iron. Slip over the cushion pad.

Bedtime bliss

Make sure all your dreams are sweet ones by trimming pillowcases and comforter covers with candy-colored ribbons and bows. Or if that's a bit too feminine for your taste, choose from the wide array of ribbons and braids on sale in fabric stores to reflect your own style. How about masculine plaids or sumptuous jewel-colored velvets instead? Plain white bed linen is just crying out for that personal touch.

1 To decorate pillowcases, choose a selection of wide and narrow ribbon or braid and ready-made bows. Cut the ribbon slightly longer than the width of the pillowcase and pin in place, turning under the ends to neaten. Machine sew close to the ribbon edges using matching thread. Alternatively, sew small ready-made bows to the pillowcase, spacing them evenly. If you wish, sew ribbons to the open edges of the case and tie in bows.

2 To decorate a comforter cover to match, choose narrow ribbon in four different colors. Cut the ribbon into 16-inch lengths, knot each piece in the center and tie into a neat bow. Pin the bows to the comforter and sew the knots in place, taking care not to sew through both layers of the cover.

Soft option

Snuggle up with cushion covers made from soft, stretchy fleece fabric. Vibrant colors add warmth to a light-colored sofa and, since fleece fabric doesn't fray, it's easy to combine a mix of contrasting hues to create bold appliqué designs.

1 Measure your cushion pad and cut green fabric for the cover front—don't allow extra for seams as the cover will stretch to fit. Cut a panel of gray fabric about 6 inches wide to fit across the front, and an orange strip 1 × 8 1/2 inches.

2 Pin the orange strip along the center of the gray panel. Using orange thread and a medium zigzag stitch on your machine, stitch the strip in place by sewing close to, but not over, its edges. Pin then stitch the gray panel onto the center of the cover front, using the same zigzag stitch and matching thread.

3 For the back, cut two panels of green fabric, each the same width as the front cover in one direction and two-thirds of the width in the other. Stitch a 3/4-inch hem along one longer edge of each. Lay out the cover front, appliqué side up, then place the back pieces on top, right side down, aligning raw edges with those of the front and overlapping hemmed edges at the center. Pin then stitch the front and backs together with a 1/4-inch seam allowance. Trim one layer of the allowance and clip corners, then turn right side out. Iron seams flat, using a cool setting, and insert the cushion pad.

TIP
The stretchiness of fleece fabric can make it difficult to cut to size, so you may find it easier to make paper patterns for the cover and appliqué pieces.

Patch it up

A patchwork throw will bring a touch of traditional charm to any bedroom. You don't need to spend hours hand-stitching tiny pieces of fabric; with large squares the sewing machine can do all the work. These instructions make a throw of about 43 × 59 inches.

1 Cut 8 1/2-inch squares from cardboard to make patterns, and use to cut seven squares from each of five coordinating fabrics. Arrange the squares right side up in rows of five across and seven down, alternating the fabrics.

2 Stitch each horizontal row of squares together into a strip, with right sides facing and 1/4-inch seam allowances. Iron seam allowances open. Lay the strips right side up in their correct positions. Pin them together, pinning through the corresponding vertical seam lines to make sure they match. Stitch the strips together.

3 For the border, cut two 2 3/4 × 56 inch strips and two 2 3/4 × 44 inch strips from a sixth fabric. With right sides facing, stitch a long strip to each long edge of the rectangle, with 1/4-inch seam allowances. Next, stitch a shorter strip to each short edge and across the tops of the borders already stitched.

4 Cut a 44 × 60 inch piece of backing fabric. With right sides facing, lay the patchwork on it and pin together around all edges. Trim any excess backing, then stitch, leaving a gap in one edge. Snip across seam allowances at the corners and turn right side out. Iron edges flat and slip stitch the gap.

TIP
For the best results with patchwork, use closely woven fabrics that are all of equal weights—printed cottons are ideal for this throw.

Feet first

Sink your toes into a luxurious bath mat. Quilted to give it a springy feel, this mat is lined with stick-on thick fleece, available from fabric stores. With the fleece stuck to one piece of toweling, it's easy to keep the layers together when sewing the quilting. Striped cotton finishes the edges with a neat border.

1 Cut two pieces of toweling

and one piece of thick fleece, each measuring 21 × 29 1/2 inches. Following the manufacturer's instructions, stick fleece to one piece of toweling. With the fleece sandwiched between them, place the two pieces of toweling together and tack 2 inches from the edges to mark the border area.

2 With the fused side up, use tailor's chalk to draw a diagonal line between opposite corners. Tack or pin near this line, then machine stitch along it, starting and ending just inside the border. Pin and stitch parallel diagonal lines 4 3/4 inches apart, then repeat in the other direction, to make a diamond pattern.

3 From contrasting cotton fabric, cut two 7 × 29 1/2 inch and two 7 × 26 1/4 inch strips. With right sides facing, stitch the long strips to the long edges of the mat, 2 inches from the edge. Press under 1/2 inch on the loose edges, fold to reverse of mat and slip stitch to the machine stitches. With the short strips extending 1/2 inch beyond each end, bind the short edges in the same way. Tuck under and slip stitch ends.

Splash catcher

Hand towels sewn together patchwork-style make a distinctive shower curtain. Pick up a bundle of towels at bargain prices at the sales, choosing two contrasting colors for a simple but striking effect. Back them with a cheap. solid-color shower curtain liner to make sure the finished result is waterproof.

1 Lay out the towels in a checkerboard pattern, overlapping the edges slightly. Towels have a nap, or pile, which can affect the depth of color, so make sure this runs in the same direction on all the towels of the same color. To check, run your hand up and down them and one direction will feel rough, the other smooth. Pin and topstitch each horizontal row together, then stitch the rows to one another, aligning the vertical seams.

2 Fold the top edge of the curtain 2 inches to the wrong side and insert eyelets following the manufacturer's instructions. Space them evenly, adjusting the spacing if necessary to avoid the seams.

3 With wrong sides facing, lay out the shower curtain liner on the toweling curtain, lining up the eyelets. Trim the liner so is is the same width as your toweling curtain and slightly shorter. Hang the curtain with hooks or rings through both sets of eyelets.

TIP
Towels are thick to sew, so use a heavy-duty needle in your sewing machine, such as a jeans needle.

Bath attendant

A toweling and gingham slipcover turns a plain chair into practical and attractive bathroom seating. Buttoned tabs mean this cover can easily be removed for washing.

1 Make a pattern by placing paper on the chair seat and creasing it along the edges. Use a ruler to draw the crease lines, then use a square ruler to draw a 4 3/4-inch skirt from each line. The corners are cut away, so the final pattern should look like a squat cross. Add 1/4-inch seam allowances to the cut-away corners, cut out the pattern and use it to cut one cover from toweling and one from lining.

2 Cut eight 2 3/4 × 7 inch tabs with pointed ends from gingham, and four from interfacing. Fuse interfacing tabs to wrong side of four gingham tabs. For binding, cut 2 1/4-inch-wide bias strips of gingham. Iron long edges 1/2 inch to wrong side.

3 With right sides facing, stitch tabs together in pairs, leaving unpointed ends open. Trim corners, turn right side out and press flat. Work an 8 1/2-inch buttonhole on each, starting 1 inch from the point. Pin tabs to front and back skirts, matching raw edges. With right sides facing and a 1/4-inch seam allowance, stitch toweling to lining at each cut-away corner, catching in tabs. Snip diagonally into seam allowances at corners. Turn to right side and iron flat.

4 Tack cover to lining at loose skirt edges. Open out binding strips. With right sides facing, raw edges matching and binding extending 1/4 inch beyond skirt ends, pin binding strips to skirt edges and stitch along fold line. Fold pressed edges of binding to lining side and slip stitch to machine stitches, tucking in ends at corners. Sew on buttons to hold tabs in place.

Easy elegance

Very little sewing is needed to create these luxurious bolster covers, since the fabric is simply knotted at the ends for a decorative effect. Silks in bright colors create a sumptuous feel. Choose silk that's the right weight so it is fine enough to knot easily yet has enough body to make the ends frill out attractively.

1 To measure how long the cover needs to be, pin silk around your bolster pad, allowing plenty of excess fabric at one end. Mark the point where the bolster ends using tailor's chalk, then knot the excess fabric. leave enough fabric beyond the knot to form a flamboyant frill and make another mark at the end of the frill. It's best to allow a bit too much at this stage, since a frill that is too small will spoil the effect; you can always trim it later. Measure between the two marks to find the length of each end section. Multiply this by two, then add the length of the bolster pad plus 1 1/2 inch for hems, to find the overall length of the cover. To find the width, measure around your bolster pad and add 1 inch for seams. Cut silk to these dimensions.

2 Fold the fabric in half lengthwise and sew the two long edges together with a 1/2-inch seam allowance to create a fabric tube. Turn up and stitch 1/4-inch double hems at each end. Place the bolster pad inside, position it and knot the fabric at both ends.

TIP
Use the whole width of the fabric and you won't have to hem the ends, as the silk should already be finished at the side edges.

Fern favourite

Customize a linen table runner with an elegant fern motif, applied using silver foil. The silver blends beautifully with this icy blue, adding a sophisticated glimmer to a simple glass-topped table. This effect could also be used to give plain comforter sets or ready-made curtains a dazzling revamp. The fern motif is created by using a prepared stencil, but if you feel artistic you can design your own, or even apply the glue and foil freehand.

1 Lay one end of the runner out on a flat surface and position the stencil on top. Hold it in place with masking tape, then dab all over the cut-out areas with appliqué glue. Leave to dry for one hour only.

2 Place a sheet of appliqué foil over the motif and rub it in firmly so that it adheres to the glue. Remove and reposition the foil sheet until the whole of the motif has been covered. Repeat the process to make a second metallic motif on the other end of the runner. When ironing, always press on the wrong side.

Smart set

Have the most stylish table settings in town with placemats that are sure to impress your guests. Complete with their own cutlery pockets, these have the luxurious look of real suede. They are simple to sew, and although the "sued"' looks expensive, it is, in fact, a realistic lookalike that is more affordable and widely available from fabric stores.

1 For each mat, cut out a piece of faux suede measuring about 10 1/4 × 12 1/2 inches. Iron and stitch a double 1/4-inch hem around the edges to create a neat, soft line. Miter the corners to make the hem sit flat. To do this, fold under the whole corner on the diagonal before hemming, and trim off most of the triangle, leaving just 1/4 inch from the diagonal fold line. Then, when you turn under the 1/4-inch double hems on the straight sides, their ends should meet neatly at the corner.

2 To make the cutlery pocket, cut another piece of fabric measuring 5 × 6 3/4 inches. Press under 1/4-inch around all edges and stitch across the top edge to hem. Position the pocket on the mat and stitch around the remaining three sides.

TIP
White linen napkins and plain white tableware will reinforce this look of stylish simplicity. Make matching napkin rings by tying the napkins with a piece of brown ribbon.

Color boost

Cheer up mealtimes with a dash of color by using dyes to give your table linen a lift. Once a boring beige, this raffia placemat is now an eye-popping pink, and there are many more color ranges to choose from. Cold water hand dyes are available from fabric and craft stores, and work best on natural fibers.

1 Weigh the mat to work out how much dye is required, according to instructions printed on the package of hand dye. Then wash the mat—you will dye it while it's still damp.

2 To mix the dye, put on rubber gloves and empty the packet of dye into a large glass container, such as a measuring cup. Add hot water according to the package directions and stir well. Fill a second, shallow container, large enough to hold the unfolded mat, with 1 1/2 gallons hot water (the temperature should be about 140°C) and 8 oz salt. Add the dye solution and stir well.

3 Submerge the damp mat in the dye bath, then agitate and squeeze it at regular intervals to make sure the color penetrates all the way through. After an hour, rinse the mat under a cold running water until the water runs clear. Wash separately with a mild, color-safe detergent.

TIP
If you want to change the color of larger items, such as a tablecloth, you may find it easier to choose a dye that can be used in your washing machine.

Simply groovy

A familiar sight on hippie T-shirts, tie-dying can also create brilliant patterns on home furnishings. Take a plain white tablecloth in a fine, even-weave natural fabric, and have fun pleating, tying and knotting to make a combination of designs. Choose any dye color you like, although patterns show up best against stronger shades, such as this indigo.

1 Most fabrics have a finish that must be removed before they can be dyed. To do this, wash in warm water with mild detergent (some fabrics, such as cotton, may have to be boiled before they will lose their finish). Leave the cloth to dry, then iron. Weigh it to find out how much dye you need—see dye package for quantities.

2 Pleat, tie or knot the fabric to create the patterns you want. For small circles, tie stones or marbles into the fabric, or for larger circles, draw the fabric into a peak and bind with thread. Make the border around the edge by pleating the fabric and placing paper clips side by side over the fold. The pattern on top is formed by pinning folds of fabric with safety pins.

3 When all the tying is done, wet the fabric thoroughly. Prepare the dye following the manufacturer's instructions and, wearing rubber gloves, submerge the cloth in the dye. Leave for up to an hour, stirring regularly.

4 Remove the cloth and rinse in cold water until the water runs clear. Wash in warm water and detergent. Remove the ties and hang the tablecloth out to dry.

TIP
Although dyed items will be colorfast, it is safer to wash them separately the first few times after dyeing to remove any color residue.

Breakfast news

Ditch the tablecloth, and instead give yourself something to read while munching your toast and cereal. Decorate your tabletop with newspaper cuttings, postcards or pages cut from an old book —how about a cook book for some culinary inspiration? If you and your family always sit in the same places, you could include a name at each place setting. If you have chairs with smooth wooden backs, try decorating them to match.

1 Gather the materials you want to paper the table with, then decide how you want to arrange them. Using a paintbrush, apply white all-purpose glue to the back of each piece. Stick them in place on the tabletop, overlapping the edges to give perfect coverage. Continue them down over the side edges of the table, wiping away excess glue immediately.

2 When the table is completely covered, leave until the glue is dry. To protect the paperwork, apply one or more coats of clear acrylic varnish to the entire surface, ensuring it is dry between coats.

Checkmate

An unassuming wooden chair gets a personality boost with some lively mosaic-style paint job. Choose a selection of complementary shades that suit your room's color scheme to paint a checkerboard design on a flat or curved chair back. You could use the same idea to jazz up a cupboard front or tabletop.

1 Sand the back of the chair, and apply undercoat. When this is dry, paint it with two coats of your lightest color, using satin finish paint. Measure the chair back and work out how many 1-inch squares will fit across and down (if it does not divide exactly, adjust the size of the squares to fit). Mark out the squares using a ruler and pencil, continuing them over the edges of the back. If your chair has a curved back, use a flexible ruler.

2 Using a square-ended artist's brush, apply the remaining colors in a random pattern. Working from the lightest to the darkest, apply one color at a time, painting all the squares in that shade and leaving them to dry before starting on the next. Wash the brush well between colors. When the last set of squares is dry, apply two coats of clear matt acrylic varnish to finish.

TIP
Since you only need small amounts of each shade, buy small quart cans of satin finish paint or, for all except the basecoat, tubes of concentrated artist's acrylics.

Shore thing

Conjure up memories of fresh sea air and walks along the coast by recreating a little patch of stone beach in your own home. Take a collection of smooth, flat pebbles and use them to make an unusual decorative tabletop. The pebbles are arranged in a metal tray mounted on a stand, where they are set in plaster of Paris.

1 If your tray is too deep, place a sheet of particle board in the base. Choose flat pebbles, wash and dry them thoroughly if

collected from the beach, and arrange them in the tray. Glue the stones one by one onto the particle board or tray base using strong epoxy adhesive. Leave the glue to harden thoroughly.

2 Cover your work surface with newspaper and mix plaster of Paris in a bowl to the consistency of cream. Pour this between the pebbles until it comes halfway up them, filling in all the spaces. Wipe off spills on the stone with a damp cloth immediately. Leave overnight to harden, then clean off any drips with steel wool.

3 Finish by applying two coats of polyurethane varnish with a soft paintbrush— use matt varnish for the white stones and satin on the dark ones, to bring out the colors.

Quick silver

Make inexpensive wooden chairs shine with a few coats of silver spray paint, and they'll look classy enough for any dining room. With the money you save on the chairs, splurge on a glass-topped table and some stylish new chrome accessories to create a cool, contemporary look.

1 Make sure the surface of your chair is clean and dry. Sand smooth furniture that has been previously painted or varnished, or give new wood two coats of primer.

2 To apply the spray paint, work outdoors or in a well-ventilated room where you have plenty of space.

Cover the surrounding area with a tarp or lots of newspapers. For the best results, apply three light coats of silver or chrome spray paint; don't be tempted to cut corners by using one heavy coat. Leave until thoroughly dry, then buff the painted surface with a soft cloth to bring up the shine.

TIP
Hints of soft pink will warm up a silver color scheme. Add bought seat pads covered in pink fabric or make your own, using foam as the base.

Stripe it bright

Adding a patterned element can lift even the most boring room out of the doldrums, and jazzing up a plain tabletop can do a lot to cheer up a dreary kitchen—without the need for major redecoration of walls or units. Stripes in complementary shades give a bright, modern look, and are easy to paint onto a plain wooden table. Yellow is an ideal choice for instant cheer, guaranteed to raise the spirits.

1 If possible, choose a table with a surface that is untreated (that is, unwaxed and unvarnished). Otherwise, sand down the surface before you start to provide a surface for the paint, then apply a basecoat of water-based paint in a light, neutral color and leave to dry.

2 Apply masking tape of varying widths down the length of the table, making sure that the lines are straight. Using a quart can of yellow and white water-based paint, paint stripes between the tapes. Leave until thoroughly dry, then carefully remove the tape. To finish, apply two coats of clear acrylic varnish.

TIP
To skip the chore of sanding down old furniture, apply a multi-surface primer. These are designed to cover any previous finish and provide a paintable surface.

Leather look

Dress up a cheap wooden table in a leather jacket and it will be able to strut its stuff in the most stylish of room settings. As well as giving the furniture a more expensive look, leather has a luxuriously tactile surface. Dark leather would suit a period-style room, but white blends in well with light, contemporary interiors. The base and legs of this plain wooden table have been painted white to match. Upholstery tacks with a bronze finish add a decorative finishing touch around the edges.

1 Cut a piece of leather that is large enough to cover your table and also wrap over its edges. Lay it on top of the table, positioning it in the center, then fold one side over the edge and fix to the underside using a staple gun or tacks. Pull the opposite edge taut and secure in the same way. Repeat with the remaining two sides, trimming excess leather at the corners and folding them neatly in place.

2 Decorate the edge of the table by hammering in a row of evenly-spaced upholstery tacks.

Appear in print

Painting designs on plywood is easy if you use mono-printing. This simple technique involves painting shapes onto acetate and then printing them onto a surface. Etching designs in the wet paint, or scrubbing it to add texture, enables you to create interesting effects. These rectangular shapes were printed using three shades of blue for a cool, fresh look.

1 Seal an unfinished plywood table with two coats of acrylic gloss varnish. In separate bowls, prepare three paint shades by mixing white water-based paint with small amounts of artist's acrylics. Using one shade, paint a shape on a sheet of acetate. To add texture, scrub the paint hard with a household paintbrush while still wet.

2 Position the acetate, paint side down, on the table. Smooth over the back to transfer the paint to the wood. Work quickly

before the paint dries. Then carefully peel back the acetate to reveal the print.

3 Print more shapes using the other shades. To decorate some with spirals or wavy lines, paint the acetate, then mark the design in the wet paint using the end of a rubber-handled brush. Apply to the table as before. Add further interest by including similar shapes in different sizes and by partially overlapping some of the blocks of color.

4 When the paint is dry, varnish the tabletop and legs with two coats of acrylic varnish.

Clever cube

Whether you use it as a footstool, coffee table or extra seating, this handsome cube will be a versatile addition to your living room. Cover a block of foam rubber with fake suede fabric and you've got a cube that looks just like the trendy leather or suede versions available in the shops —but at a fraction of the price.

1 Ask a foam supplier to cut a cube to size for you—this one measures 20 inches square. From faux suede fabric, cut a square the same size as one side of the cube, adding 3 inches for seam allowances. Using this as a template, cut four more squares.

2 With the right sides of the fabric facing, sew the five squares together to make a cross shape. Iron flat the seam allowances. Sew the four side seams to form an open cube. Trim seam allowances and turn the cube right side out. If the fabric is the type that frays badly, hem the four raw edges. Squeeze the foam inside the fabric cube.

3 To make a firm base, place a square of stiff board on top of the foam. Pull the raw or hemmed fabric edges taut over the board and secure them in place using a staple gun. Use the cube with the board at the bottom.

Cabinet reshuffle

This pretty cupboard looks like a hand-painted piece that has stood the test of time, but in fact its aged look is the result of a distressed paint effect, and the floral design on the door has been applied using transfer glaze. This clever substance enables you to choose any picture you like and reproduce it on another surface simply by brushing on the glaze to form a transfer.

1 Sand down your cabinet to remove any previous finish, then paint it all over with a mid-tone shade of green or blue. Leave to dry, then rub candlewax on areas that might suffer wear and tear, such as the panel edges. Apply a coat of white or cream paint on top. Then, when dry, rub back the waxed areas with fine steel wool to expose glimpses of the colored base coat.

2 To create the image, find a picture you like. This should be on paper and the right size to cover the front of the cabinet—enlarge it using a color photocopier if necessary. Paint transfer glaze over the face of your picture, brushing it on vertically. When dry, add another coat, applied horizontally. Add two more coats, one in each direction, then leave to dry for two hours.

3 Soak the image in warm water, with the print face down, for 20 minutes. Then remove the print and place it face down on the cupboard door. Peel the paper away using your fingertips, leaving the image and glaze behind. Seal by painting over the image with more transfer glaze.

TIP
If you prefer a top coat in a darker color, simply reverse the order in which the shades are applied, using white or cream as a contrasting base coat.

Second sitting

Re-upholstering a drop-in seat pad can give an old chair a new lease on life. You'll need a hammer and small tacks or a staple gun.

1 Remove the seat pad and use a chisel or pliers to pry out any tacks or staples securing the existing fabric. If the pad is damaged, replace it with new foam cut to size. If not, brush it down. Measure the seat pad, taking the tape measure right around to the wooden frame. Cut a template from tracing paper, adding 2 inches all around, and use to cut this shape from padding, ticking and upholstery fabric.

2 Lay the ticking out and place the padding then the seat pad on top. Starting from the center back, fold the ticking up onto the frame and staple or tack in the center of each side. Making sure the fabric is straight, staple or tack all along one edge, working from the center out.

Repeat on the opposite edge, pulling the fabric taut. Secure adjoining sides, then trim padding and ticking back to the tacks or staples.

3 Repeat step 2 using the upholstery fabric. At the corners, fold the fabric into neat miters, checking that it's smooth on top.

4 Cut ticking to cover the base of the seat pad and press under 1/4 inch around all edges. Tack or staple in place on the underside of the pad. Replace seat pad in the chair.

TIP
Choose durable, fire-proof fabrics that will keep their shape when stretched taut.

Twenties revival

Re-create the glamorous mirrored fashions of the 1920s by adding a reflective top to a pretty period-style table. Look for a suitable piece of furniture in a junk shop or from unfinished furniture suppliers. You can create the exact look you want by giving the table a complete makeover with a bit of paint and a beautiful new drawer handle, as well.

1 If you are revamping a table that is varnished or polished, either sand it down well to provide a surface for the paint, or apply a coat of multi-surface primer. Paint every surface, except those to be covered with mirrors, with satin finish paint in the color of your choice.

2 Measure or make a template of the surfaces to be mirrored —the top of the table and the front of the drawer. Ask a local glazier to cut pieces of mirror to the required sizes, and also to polish the edges and drill a hole for a drawer handle. Apply mirror glue (ask at your glazier or home improvement store) to the tabletop and drawer front and press the mirrors into position. Leave to dry for at least 24 hours, then attach the drawer handle.

Deck 'em out

If your old deck chair covers are looking faded or tattered, brighten up summer days by making some crisp new ones that simply slip over the top. That means you don't have to spend time removing the old covers or hand-stitching the new ones to the wooden frame. When the slipcovers need to be washed, all you have to do is open the Velcro fastening and whip them off. Choose tightly woven cotton prints for the best results.

1 Measure the length and width of the existing cover, then cut fabric to the same width plus 1 1/2 inches, and twice the length plus 3 inches. If the fabric you choose is more than twice the width of the cover, you can economize by cutting it in half lengthwise and stitching the two pieces together to make the required length. Press under and stitch a double 1/4-inch hem around all edges.

2 Stitch corresponding strips of Velcro to the wrong side of one short end and the right side of the other end. Loop over the existing cover and secure the Velcro ends together.

Light relief

Bring a new dimension to stencilling by adding spackle to the paint, giving designs a raised, textured finish. Forget fussy flowers and grapevines; this treatment works best with simple, modern motifs such as this abstract leaf design, used to add an eye-catching border around an alcove.

1 Trace a motif onto paper using a soft pencil. Turn the paper over and thickly trace over the outline on the back. Place paper, with this back side down, on a sheet of waxed stencil card. Go over the outline to transfer the image onto the card. Place the card on a board or a thick layer of newspaper and carefully cut out the motif using a sharp craft knife.

2 Mix powdered spackle with a little water so it has a thick and creamy texture, then add acrylic paint in the shade of your choice, a little at a time, until you're happy with the color. Bear in mind that when dry the mixture will look slightly lighter than when wet.

3 Plan the layout of the motifs on the wall, using a level and ruler to line them up evenly. Tape the stencil lightly to the wall and apply the colored spackle over the cutout areas with a short-bristled brush or palette knife. Use a gentle stippling movement so the spackle stands up in peaks. Carefully peel back the stencil to reveal the motif. If spackle has bled underneath, allow it to dry, then carefully scratch away with the tip of a craft knife.

TIP
Relief stencilling can also be used to jazz up plain, unglazed tiles. In a bathroom or kitchen, protect your work from steam and moisture by applying a coat of acrylic spray varnish.

Floor show

If you want to give wooden floorboards a livelier look, a bit of paint is the answer. The lines of the boards suggest a ready-made pattern, so choose two contrasting shades of satin finish and use them to create dramatic stripes. To avoid too regimented an effect, vary the width of the stripes from one to three boards.

1 To prepare your floorboards, hammer down any protruding nails and rub down sharp edges and splinters. If you have sanded bare boards, apply wood filler over the knots, then add a coat of wood primer. When dry, rub down with fine wet-and-dry sandpaper to remove blemishes and wipe over using a cloth dampened with turpentine. Fill any gaps with wood filler. If your boards are varnished, stained or already painted, simply sand the surface, then clean with warm soapy water before painting.

2 Measure your room and count the number of floorboards. Draw a scale version of your design on graph paper—plan the spacing between the stripes by using the boards as a guide.

3 On the floor, mask off all the stripes to be painted in your first color. Apply two coats of the first paint shade. When this is dry, carefully remove the masking tape. Mask off the remaining boards, apply two coats of the second color and, when dry, remove the masking tape.

4 Finally, apply two coats of a suitable clear floor varnish to protect the design from wear and tear, leaving it to dry thoroughly between each coat. Do not walk on the floor until it is completely dry.

TIP
Use low-tack masking tape—this will not lift off the paint you have already applied when you mask off the second set of boards.

Rock star

Pebbles and plaster create a fireplace that combines classic drama with more rustic elements. A pair of ornate corbels forms an intriguing contrast with the simple wood mantel shelf, painted and distressed to resemble driftwood. Corbels are available in a wide range of styles, and may be made of wood or plaster, so you can be as plain or elaborate as you want. The unfinished brick interior of the fireplace adds to the rustic appeal, while a semi-circle of concrete set with pebbles makes an attractive hearth.

1 Cut a length of wood to size for the mantel shelf and sand down the edges and corners to give a worn look. Paint the timber with white water-based paint then, when dry, rub away patches of the paint with fine steel wool to create a distressed appearance. Fix the shelf to he wall above the fireplace using brackets.

2 Paint the corbels white using fire-resistant paint. When dry, place one corbel over each bracket and glue and screw in place.

3 To make a mold for the pebbly hearth, cut a piece of curved plastic to the width of the hearth, plus at least 6 inches on either side. Screw in place at each side of the fireplace opening. Pour in concrete until it's level with the plastic and embed a selection of dark and light pebbles in the surface. Leave for 24 hours to set, then remove the mold.

Clear winner

If your bedroom is on the small side, a separate dressing area may seem out of the question. But with this stylish screen you can create an effective partition without losing light. Clear Plexiglas is decorated with a square design using etching spray, which creates a finish that looks like frosted glass. The result will provide a degree of privacy for a dressing area, or conceal the chaos of your sewing corner or office space, without making the room seem smaller or darker.

1 Take a sheet of clear Plexiglas, cut to the size you want—your supplier may be able to do this for you. Cover the Plexiglas with a grid design of evenly sized squares by sticking on strips of masking tape.

2 Coat the screen all over with etching spray. Work in a well-ventilated area and cover the surrounding surfaces well with a tarp or newspaper. Spray on two or three light coats, building up the coverage gradually until you achieve the effect you want. Leave to dry.

3 Remove the masking tape to reveal the design. Drill small holes at the top of the screen and hang from the ceiling using lengths of fine chain.

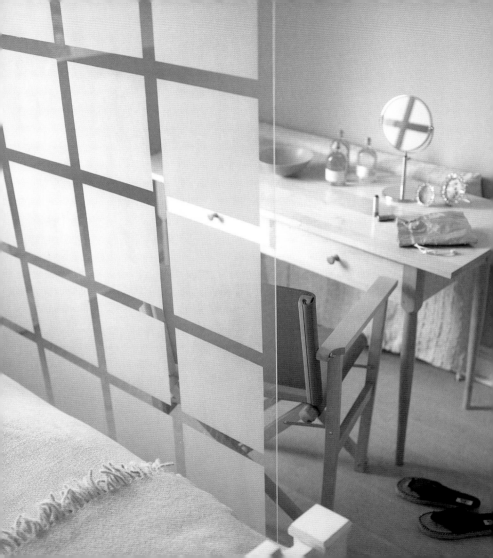

Stamp duty

Sometimes plain walls need more than a few pictures to liven them up, but if you can't face grappling with wallpaper, try stamping. With this nifty paint effect, you can cover a large area in a jiffy, adding as few or as many motifs as you like. You'll find a wide range of rubber stamps in art, craft and home improvement stores, which should also sell the tiny roller you need to apply the paint to the stamp. You can buy special stamp paints, but regular water-based paint is fine for walls and ceilings—quart cans go a long way.

1 Clean the wall using a soft scrubbing brush, and dry with a soft cloth. Pour a small amount of paint onto an old plate. Push the roller through the paint, then roll it over the raised surface of the stamp in a thin, even coat. Avoid applying too much as the stamp may smudge, or too little as the resulting image may be patchy.

If paint seeps off the edge of the raised motif, clean it up with a cotton swab.

2 Carefully press the stamp onto the wall. To make sure you get even coverage, gently rock the stamp in all directions, taking care not to smudge the design. Lift the stamp away as evenly as possible. If you make a mistake while stamping, wipe away wet paint with a clean, damp cloth. If the print doesn't come out completely the first time, fill in details using a small artist's brush. Be sure to wash and dry your stamp between each application.

TIP
For a coordinated look, try stamping lampshades and cushion fabrics with the same design using fabric paint.

Little gems

Just a few handmade or designer tiles can make an amazing difference to a wall of plain standard-issue ones, and making them yourself guarantees a unique look. These glittering tiles will add an air of glamour to any bathroom. They are created by casting plaster in a simple home-made mold and are set with a mix of sparkling glass beads and ordinary pebbles. Choose beads in colors that complement your room, and pick up pebbles from your garden for a truly personal touch.

1 To make a mold, cut four 6 3/4-inch lengths of 1 1/2 × 3/4 inch plywood. Place them on 1-inch thick flexible board to make a 1 1/2-inch-high box. Firmly fix the outer corners with masking tape.

2 Following the manufacturer's instructions, mix some plaster and, as it thickens, pour into the mold. Place a selection of pebbles and beads on top, arranging them in a circle. Leave the plaster until it has set, then take off the battens and flex the board to dislodge the tile.

3 Place a few of the finished tiles at random among a wall of plain white ones or use them to make a border or backsplash; you don't need many to add instant glamour.

Panel games

If you've ever craved a wood-paneled library effect in a sitting room or study, it's easy to create the look with a few pieces of wood. Particle board planks up to about 6 inches wide can simply be glued to the wall to form a grid and, when painted to blend in with the background color, they create the illusion of period-style paneling. For a more informal paneled effect, glue just a few planks to the lower part of a wall. This is a good way to add interest to a boring hallway and protect the walls from the wear and tear of daily traffic. The planks in the inset picture are made of softwood and tinted with wood stain.

1 Measure your wall and decide on the height and width of the panels. Remember to allow for the fact that you need to end with a plank of wood along each edge of the wall. Using a level and a pencil, mark the positions of the horizontal planks on the wall, so that you get each piece of wood straight. Mark the positions for the vertical planks using a plumbline, again to help you get them straight.

2 Cut 1 1/2-inch thick particle board planks to size and glue them to the wall using strong wood glue. When the glue has dried, paint the entire wall with two coats of water-based paint.

TIP
Stick your paneling onto a wall lined with wallpaper and it will be easy to remove if you want to change the look.

Square deal

Walls covered in checks can add pattern and pace to a room, but they may also overpower a small space if the contrast between the colors is too great. If you like the look but want to avoid making your room look like a chess board, try a more subtle approach. Using two similar shades creates a less garish effect, while choosing gloss finish for one color and matte for the other creates a variation in texture as well as tone. Blue is a perfect color for this project, because its different shades blend harmoniously.

1 Paint the whole wall using the lighter paint shade in matte finish water-based paint. When this is dry, lightly mark out squares on your wall using a pencil and ruler, enlisting the help of a level and plumbline to help you get the lines straight.

2 Mask off alternate squares using low-tack masking tape and paint these in a slightly darker shade of glossy water-based paint. When the paint is dry, carefully peel away the tape. Check for any stray pencil marks and remove using a soft, clean eraser.

Climbing plants

A rambling stencil in a soft color applied over a neutral base gives the look of expensive hand painted wallpaper. To cover a wall, you will need a repeat stencil, which is designed to create a seamless look. Buy a pre-cut stencil; if you choose a less intricate design the stencil company may offer a cheaper one you can cut out yourself, but if you're decorating a large area it's worth paying for a ready-cut version. For an even finish, use a tiny sponge roller instead of a brush to paint the design.

1 Make sure your wall is flat and free of cracks and blemishes. Paint the wall with water-based paint in a light, neutral shade and leave to dry.

2 Cover the back of the stencil with a light spray adhesive that allows you to easily reposition and remove the stencil. Position it in a top corner of the wall, checking that it is straight. Pour some contrasting color paint onto an old plate and cover the sponge roller with paint, taking care not to overload it. Pass the roller over the stencil, pressing firmly and evenly until all details of the design are covered with paint.

3 Lightly mark a pencil dot in each of the registration holes on the stencil to ensure that the next design aligns exactly. Move the stencil to the next position and repeat the process until the wall has been covered.

TIP
It's a good idea to cover your wall with plain wallpaper before painting to create a perfectly smooth surface for stenciling.

124

Silver lining

Take a shine to metal leaf and you'll see just how easy it can be to glamorize your walls and accessories. Great for adding a touch of glitz around your home, metal leaf is sold as fine sheets of gold or silver attached to a backing sheet. Cheaper versions of less precious metals are also available and look equally as stunning. These silvery squares, for example, are created using aluminum leaf. To apply the leaf, you will need a special glue called size and a soft brush to smooth it in place. It's best to use gold and silver effects in moderation, as overdoing them can look tacky rather than terrific. A couple of columns of silver squares used to highlight the wall near a dining area can enrich a whole room.

1 Use a ruler and pencil to mark the lines of the design on the wall, then mask off each of the squares using low-tack masking tape.

2 Brush a little metal size onto one of the squares on the wall and wait for it to become tacky, which should take about 15 minutes. Lay a sheet of metal leaf over the square and gently smooth it in place using a flat, soft brush, then remove the backing. Repeat for the remaining squares. Leave until the size is completely dry before carefully peeling away the masking tape.

Screen play

The backsplash behind the sink might have a practical job to do, but it doesn't have to be boring. So brighten up your bathroom and give yourself something to look at while brushing your teeth. You don't need fancy designer tiles—the cut-price way to add color and pattern is simply to take a piece of your favorite fabric and trap it behind a sheet of see-through acrylic. Sealing the edges keeps the fabric dry.

1 Clear acrylic sheets are available from home improvement stores. Measure the area you want to cover and ask if you can have a piece cut to your exact size. Cut a piece of fabric to match the size of your acrylic panel, taking into account the positioning of any large designs or patterns.

2 Sandwiching the fabric between the wall and the acrylic sheet, fix the panel in place using mirror-head screws. Seal around the edges with clear bathroom sealant to prevent water from seeping in and soaking the fabric.

Wrapper's delight

Give plain ceramic vases an unusual textured covering using fine cotton cord. Winding it carefully around and gluing it in place creates an attractive ribbed surface. For a more rustic look, try using seagrass, jute or twine. Choose vases with simple shapes and smooth curves.

1 Mask the exterior of the vase with newspaper, then paint the inside and the rim using fast-drying enamel spray paint in a color that contrasts with your cord. Apply it in several fine layers, leaving it to dry between coats. When the final layer is dry, remove the newspaper.

2 Coat the lower half of the vase with adhesive and leave until tacky. Use a glue that stays tacky for awhile, such as contact or heavy-duty spray adhesive. Fasten the end of the cord at the base of the vase using masking tape. Keeping the vase upright, carefully wind the cord around it, making sure each loop sits snugly against the previous one. When you're done with the lower half, apply adhesive to the upper half and keep winding.

3 When you are 1/4 inch from the top of the vase, apply a little extra adhesive to the remainder to make sure the last coils of cord are secure. When you reach the top, cut diagonally across the cord, dab a little all-purpose white glue onto the end and stick in place. Leave the glue to harden, then remove the masking tape. Using a soft brush, coat the cord with all-purpose glue diluted with an equal quantity of water, which acts as a seal.

TIP
Don't pull the cord too tight when winding, as this could cause gaps between the coils.

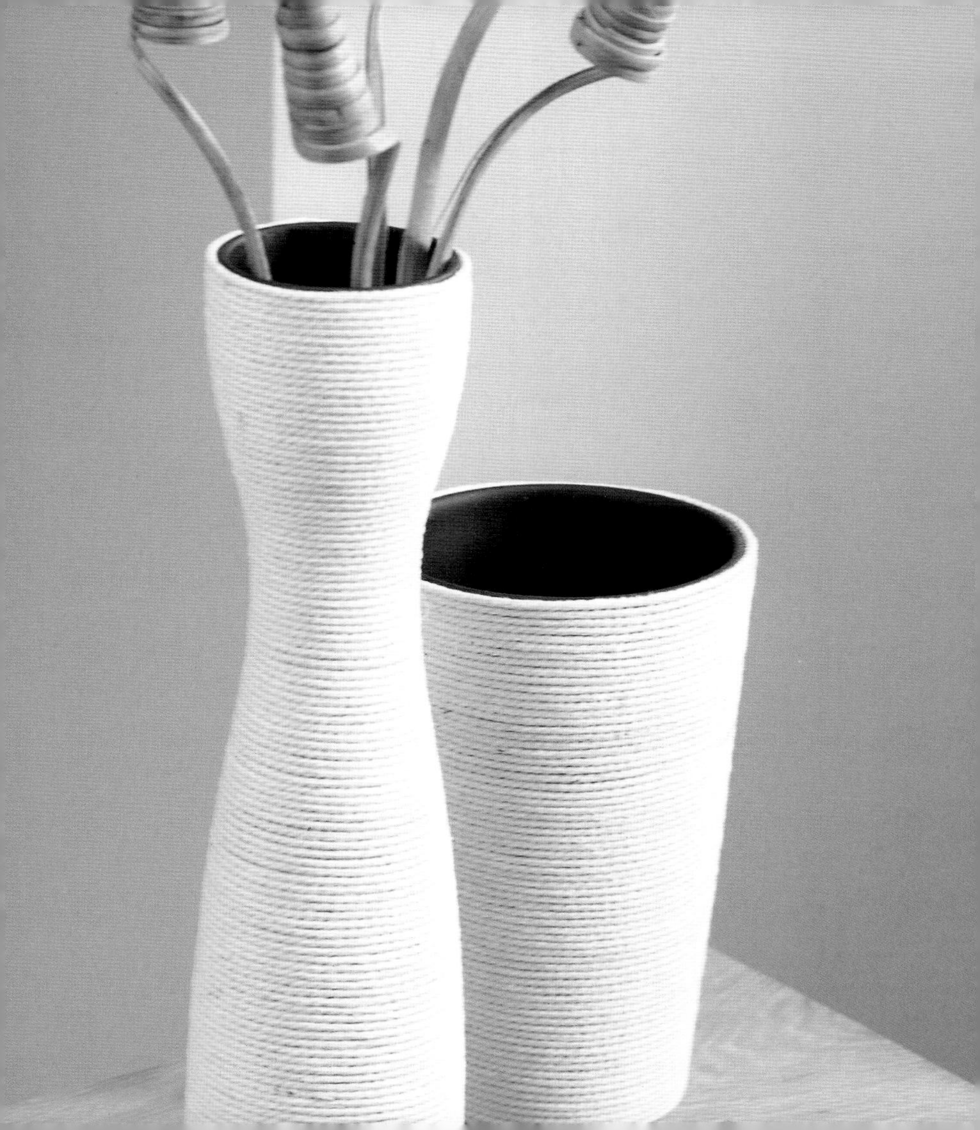

Paper work

Papier-mâché is a technique we've all tried as kids using soggy strips of newspaper, but when you replace this with delicate handmade paper, and throw in a few leaves and a bit of silver leaf, the results are worthy of a designer's studio. Look for textured paper that is fine enough to let the leaves and silver show through. You will also need wallpaper paste, a glass bowl to use as a mold and some plastic wrap to prevent the papier-mâché from sticking to the bowl.

1 Lay newspaper over your work surface, then prepare wallpaper paste following the package instructions. Cover the outside of the glass bowl with plastic wrap.

2 Tear handmade paper into strips. Coat each with paste by dipping it in then running it through your fingers to remove any excess. Smooth the strip onto the outside of the bowl.

Repeat until the bowl is covered with paper. Leave to dry.

3 When the paper is dry, place the leaves on the bowl and apply a second layer of pasted paper over the top to hold them in place. Leave to dry.

4 Add patches of silver leaf by

brushing a small amount of paste onto the bowl before carefully sticking the leaf in place. Add more layers of handmade paper until you are satisfied. When dry, separate the papier-mâché from the bowl by gently easing off the plastic wrap. If splits appear, patch them with paste-coated paper.

TIP
Make sure each layer of papier-mâché is thoroughly dry before applying the next. A blast with a hairdryer will help speed things up.

Feather report

Take glass vases from plain to exquisite with delicate images derived from real feathers. You will need access to a color photocopier, some wet release transfer paper and a collection of feathers.

1 Make color photocopies of feathers onto the glossy side of the transfer paper, at a size appropriate for the vase. Fit as many feather images as you can onto the paper, either by using the copier's stop and repeat option or by copying the feathers onto plain paper first, then recopying onto the transfer sheet.

2 Cut carefully around the feather images. Submerge each in a bowl of lukewarm water and soak for a couple of minutes until the transfer images separate easily from the backing sheet. While the images are soaking, make sure your vase is clean and lightly wet it with cold water.

3 Carefully lift the feather transfer images out of the water (leaving the backing sheet behind) and place on the wetted vase. Gently slide the transfers around the vase until you find the position you want, smoothing out wrinkles or air bubbles with a finger or sponge. Dab gently with paper towels to remove excess water.

4 Leave the vase to dry for at least an hour before handling (a hairdryer can speed things up). If your vase is likely to come into regular contact with water, spray the decoration with a light coat of polyurethane varnish to waterproof it and prevent peeling and scratching.

TIP
If you prefer, use leaves or flowers instead of feathers. When copying, protect the copier surface from pollen by placing clear acetate underneath the flowers and white paper on top.

Shell out

Set your seashore treasures in the center of homemade glycerine soaps and wait to see what gets washed up in your bath. Ideal for giving as gifts, these soaps are made by melting glycerine soap compound, available from craft shops, and then pouring it into a mold. For this, use any suitable container you may find around the house—cut-down milk cartons are ideal. You can color the soaps the shade of your choice and also add essential oils to give them fragrance.

1 Grate or slice some glycerine soap compound into thin slivers and heat gently, using an ovensafe bowl over a pan of boiling water. Be very careful not to overheat the melted soap, as it can catch fire if left unattended.

2 Add color if you like, using soap color blocks. Their coloring is very intense: This blue was achieved using only a pea-sized lump for two blocks of soap compound. Add the color very gradually and mix in well before adding more. At this stage you can also add a few drops of essential oil for fragrance.

3 Pour 1/4 inch or so of the mixture into a mold and leave for five to six minutes until almost set. Press your shell gently into it, and top with melted soap compound until the shell is covered. Leave to set, then remove from the mold.

TIP
If you can't get to a beach to pick up shells, they are widely available in stores. Be sure to buy ones that come from properly managed sustainable sources.

Metallic plant markers

Make a set of chic markers to keep tabs on pots of herbs. These shiny metallic leaves and flowers are cut from fine aluminum foil, and the embossed names and other details are simply drawn on using ballpoint pen. Add to the metallic look by displaying your plants in galvanized pots, then line them up along a shelf or windowsill.

1 Draw leaf and flower shapes on cardboard and cut out to make templates. Lay the templates on heavy aluminum foil and draw around them with a ballpoint pen. Cut out the metal shapes using small, sharp scissors.

2 Use an ballpoint pen without the ink cartridge to add markings on the petals and leaves. Write a plant name on the back of each marker, writing in reverse to create an embossed effect on the front. To transfer words in reverse to the back of foil, write them first on tracing paper, then place the tracing face down on the foil and re-draw over the lines. Glue each marker to a piece of heavy galvanized wire using an adhesive that will stick to metal.

Top of the pots

Terracotta pots cost very little at garden centers and home improvement stores and can be transformed from standard to beautiful with just a few coats of paint. These colorful planters have a bold design that contrasts deep blue and white in vertical stripes, which are easy to create using masking tape. If you feel more artistic, you can try making your own designs.

1 Make sure your pot is clean and dry, then apply undercoat and allow to dry completely. This helps the paint color stay true, as terracotta pots are quite porous. Then paint on a coat of white water-based paint and leave to dry.

2 To make the stripes, cut strips of masking tape and stick them carefully down the length of the pot, making sure they are totally flat. Paint over the whole pot again in the contrasting color of your choice. When this second coat is dry, carefully remove the tape, and apply a coat of acrylic matte varnish to protect the paintwork.

Tray chic

Serve up breakfast in bed on a colorful mosaic tray. A mixed bag of individual tiles in pretty shades of blue turns a plain base into a real wake-up call, while the rest of the tray is painted in pure white. If possible, choose a tray made from unfinished wood, which can be painted without any preparation. These are available from companies that sell unfinished furniture and basic wooden accessories.

1 Sand the base of the tray, then prime with a half-and-half mixture of all-purpose white glue and water. Gather enough mosaic tiles to cover your tray. Using a small brush, apply a blob of all-purpose glue to the rippled side of a tile, then stick in place on the base. Repeat until the area is covered, making sure you leave a gap between each tile for grout. Leave to dry overnight.

2 Mix some grout following the manufacturer's instructions. Using a squeegee, cover the tiles with grout, pressing it into the gaps and wiping off any excess with a damp sponge. When the grout is dry to the touch, polish the tiles with a soft cloth. Paint the rest of the tray with matte finish water-based paint emulsion, followed by a couple of coats of acrylic varnish, leaving each coat to dry before applying the next.

Patio partners

Add the finishing touch to a garden deck with some designer-style planters. These cool customers show off fresh white paintwork and borders of bright blue mosaic, but they started out as ordinary terracotta pots. With white gravel to complete the picture, they now have a slick, contemporary look. If your patio is more traditional in style, you may prefer to paint the pots in blues or greens that blend in with your garden.

1 Thoroughly clean a large terracotta pot, then apply two coats of white oil-based paint, continuing it over the inside of the top rim. Leave each coat to dry.

2 Buy mosaic tiles that come attached to a backing sheet and cut a strip, two tiles wide, to fit around the outside rim of the pot. Spread waterproof tile adhesive over the rim and stick on the tiles, wavy side down, leaving the paper backing attached. Leave to set according to the manufacturer's instructions. When set, dampen the backing paper with a wet sponge and peel it off. Apply waterproof grout over the tiles, using a squeegee or sponge to push it into the gaps between them.

3 Put in your soil and plant, then sprinkle white gravel over the top of the soil.

Spud craft

You may think potato prints are just child's play, but they can create some slick designs on grown-up stationery. Cut your spuds into simple shapes, such as hearts or circles, and then stamp away. These designs are painted using nail polish, so search your make-up drawer for all those too-shocking pinks and oranges that you no longer wear, and put them to good use.

1 Cut a potato in half and use a craft knife to outline a simple shape on the cut surface of each half. Cut away the potato from around the shape so that it creates a raised stamp. Dry the potato with paper towels.

2 Coat the cut shapes lightly with nail polish, then press them onto notepaper. Reapply the nail polish before stamping each motif.

Blues band

You don't need expensive vases to show off fresh flowers. Simply recycle a few shapely bottles from your kitchen cupboards, place one or two flower stems in each and group them together. Clear glass bottles look good without any further decoration, but if you want to give your display a color boost, try painting them in different shades of the same hue. Spray paints make it easy to get even coverage.

1 Clean and thoroughly dry a used vinaigrette or wine bottle. Working in a well-ventilated area, place the bottle in an open cardboard box and spray it with an even coat of enamel paint, making sure you keep the spray contained in the box.

2 Paint more bottles of various sizes in different shades of the same color, then arrange them together in a group to make a stylish display.

Sew pretty

Add a special touch to a plain toiletries bag with decorative embroidered flowers. Two simple stitches—chain and satin—are used to create a row of motifs. Before you start on the actual item, practice your stitching on a scrap of fabric.

1 Copy the outline of this simple flower design onto tracing paper and pin it, tracing side up, to the bag. Slip dressmaker's carbon paper under the tracing, carbon side down, and softly pencil over the design lines. Repeat until you have transferred a row of flower designs to the bag.

2 Thread a sharp embroidery needle—crewel size 7 is ideal—with two strands of six-strand embroidery thread in pink. Embroider the petals using satin stitch: Starting at one end of the area to be stitched, secure the thread with backstitch then, inserting the needle just outside the marked lines, work parallel stitches close together to fill in the shape. Tie off the thread at the back.

3 Using two strands of silver thread, satin stitch the leaves, then work a small dot in the center of the petals. Add the stems in chain stitch: Bring the needle up from the back of the fabric and reinsert it just beside the point at which it emerged. Bring the point of the needle out a small distance away and loop the thread under the point of the needle. Pull the needle through. Repeat to form the next loop in the chain.

TIP
If you want to work the design on a piece of fabric rather than a toiletries bag, mounting it in a small embroidery hoop will make the sewing easier.

Gold plate

Give a trio of ordinary glass plates the Midas touch and make a glamorous display for your mantelpiece. The underside of each plate is decorated with gold leaf, applied to create simple geometric designs, and some of the clear areas have been given a frosted look with etching spray. Metallic gold leaf is sold in sheets, and you can also buy it in a kit that includes the other special items you need: size (the glue used for gilding), shellac and brushes

1 Using masking tape, mark out your chosen pattern on the underside of the plate, covering the areas you don't want to gild. Using a brush, apply a thin layer of size over the rest of the underside and leave until the size becomes tacky to the touch.

2 Carefully lay a sheet of gold leaf onto the tacky surface and use a soft, flat brush to gently stroke the foil in place. Continue applying sheets until the underside of the plate is covered. Leave to dry, then remove the tape and brush away any excess leaf before buffing with a soft cloth.

3 If you want to give the non-gilded areas of your plate a frosted look, spray the back of the plate with a thin coat of etching spray. When this is dry, add a coat of shellac to seal the decoration.

TIP
If the gold leaf breaks up slightly while you are applying it, don't panic. This will only add to the handcrafted effect and texture of the decoration.

Scent sensation

These tiny sachets slip easily into a drawer or closet to fill your clothes with the fresh scent of lavender. Taking just minutes to make, they are great as last-minute stocking stuffers for Christmas. Wide ribbon is used for the body of the bag; gather together a mixture of plain and striped ribbons to create a varied selection of sachets.

1 Using ribbon that's at least 2 inches wide, cut a piece approximately 12 inches long. Hem the raw ends, then fold the ribbon in half with right sides facing so that the hemmed ends meet. Stitch down both sides, close to the edge, then turn the bag right side out.

2 Fill the sachet with dried lavender and tie at the neck with narrow ribbon. If you want to hang the sachet in a closet, tie the ends of the narrow ribbon together to make a loop.

Rustic charm

Treat a battered old tray to a facelift by covering it with burlap. This woven material has a rough natural texture, which is perfect for injecting a hint of homey country style into a kitchen. The look is completed by wrapping the handles of the tray with string.

1 Remove the handles of the tray. Cut a rectangle of burlap to cover its inner surface and edges. Cut another rectangle to fit over the base, outer edges and top edges of the tray, allowing 1/4 inch extra all round.

2 Using fabric adhesive, glue the outer piece of burlap in place over the base and edges, continuing the 1/4-inch excess down over the inside edges. Snip into the fabric at the corners and miter it neatly. Glue the other piece of fabric to the inside surface and edges, lapping it over the first piece of burlap at the top of the inner edges.

3 To seal the burlap, dilute one part all-purpose white glue with five parts water and brush it over the whole tray. Hold the fabric in place with clothes pegs while it dries, then trim away any excess fabric at the top edges. Bind the handles with brown string, then replace them on the tray.

Bejewelled

Turn plain tableware into pieces that look as if they've just popped out of a treasure chest. Glowing cabochons (shiny glass beads) can be used to glamorize the borders of plates or the rims of bowls. Although the decorated items might not stand up to the rigors of everyday wear and tear, they are great for adding a bit of extra sparkle to a special-occasion meal. This frosted glass platter and bowl, jazzed up with gold cabochons, team up to make a showy table centerpiece.

1 Take a plain ceramic or glass plate. Stick your colored glass cabochons around its perimeter using epoxy resin, arranging them in a random design.

2 Take a bowl that matches the plate. (It needs to have a wide rim that is flat at the top.) Stick a few more of the glass cabochons around the rim. Fill the bowl with small, colorful fruits or foil-wrapped candies and place it in the center of the plate to make a display for a table or sideboard.

Flower power

Give a plain glass plate a bright, summery look with colorful flower motifs. Giftwrap is a good source of designs, or you could cut some from old magazines or books. The flowers are simply pasted face down onto the underside of a clear plate, so that they can be seen through the glass, and the white background is added with enamel paint. The matching vase is decorated the same way, on the inside—remember to choose one that's large enough that you can get your hand inside. After decorating, the glassware can be washed carefully but not soaked in water.

1 Take a clear glass plate and vase, wash in detergent and leave to dry. Using sharp scissors, carefully cut out paper flower designs and position them evenly around the underside of the plate. Using paper glue, stick the flowers in place by brushing the glue onto the plate and pressing each flower in place. Smooth from center to edges to remove air bubbles, and wipe off excess glue with a damp sponge.

2 When the glue is dry, brush on a coat of clear acrylic varnish to seal. Leave to dry, then apply two or three coats of enamel paint in your chosen color all over the underside of the plate.

3 Stick more flower motifs on the inside of the vase. Seal them with varnish, then apply the enamel paint on the inside, as with the plate.

TIP
Since the vase is decorated on the inside, you will need to place another glass jar inside it if you want to use it for fresh flowers.

Designs on china

Ever thought of creating your own designs for tableware? Plain white china provides a blank canvas for painting, and it's easy if you stick to simple, geometric designs such as small blocks, stripes and dots of color. Ceramic paints that can be hardened in the oven create a durable finish on china—just check that the ones you buy are safe to eat off. Try decorating a few plates and then, if you like the results, why not go on to tackle a complete dinner service? On smaller pieces, such as cups and saucers, use a narrow brush to form fine bands of color.

1 Wash each plate in warm, soapy water to remove any grease, and dry thoroughly.

2 Using a soft, flat artist's brush, paint a border of blocks about 3/4-inch wide all around the rim of each plate. If you want a regular design, mark it out first using a china marker. If you make mistakes, you can wipe off the paint before it dries. When you've painted on all the blocks, leave to dry.

3 Use a nail or craft knife to scratch horizontal lines into the dry paint so that the white shows through. When you're happy with the design, bake the plate in the oven to fix the paint, carefully following the manufacturer's instructions.

Weighty matters

Clip this elegant ornamental weight to the corner of your tablecloth to keep it in place. It comes in especially handy if you're eating outdoors on a windy day, and makes an attractive finishing touch at any time. Mix a selection of colored beads with decorative metallic objects for a high-glamour look. You'll find a wide range of beads available, but it's fun to buy some plain glass ones and paint them with your own choice of colors and designs. Check out your local craft shop for paints and pens suitable for use on glass.

1 Wrap masking tape around one end of a cocktail stick and push a bead onto it so it is secure enough not to slip off. Repeat for other beads. Holding the stick, dip each bead into a bottle of glass paint. Shake surplus paint back into the bottle, then stick the sticks in poster putty until the paint has dried.

2 Use an outliner pen to draw designs on the beads in contrasting colors. When the paint is dry, remove the beads from the sticks and thread them onto a 4-inch length of jewelry wire attached to the base of a curtain clip. Use pliers to cut the wire ends, and push the ends into the bead centers to hide them. Hang from the corner of any tablecloth.

TIP
If you don't have any poster putty on hand, push the cocktail sticks into half a potato while the beads are drying.

Reflected glory

The flickering flame of a tealight candle casts glowing reflections in the mirrored walls of this smart, contemporary candle sconce. The simple design is easy to put together using three pieces of particle board, which are covered with mirror mosaic tiles. Mirrors are the easiest of mosaics to work with, because they need no grouting. Buy tiles sold in sheets, attached to backing paper, so that you don't have to stick them on individually.

1 From 3/4-inch-thick particle board, cut three pieces: one 4 inches square, another of 4 3/4 inches square and the third measuring 4 × 4 3/4 inches. Place them together to make the sconce and glue the edges using strong wood glue.

Seal the particle board with a mixture of half all-purpose white glue and half water. Leave to dry.

2 From a sheet of paper-backed mirror mosaic tiles, cut three 4-inch squares to cover the inner surfaces of the sconce and three 4 3/4-inch squares to cover the outer surfaces. Cut strips one tile wide to cover the edges. To fix the mosaics to the sconce, squeeze all-purpose glue onto the tiled side of the square or strip and place in position. When the sconce is covered, leave for about four hours until the glue is dry. To remove the backing paper, dampen it with a sponge and leave for several minutes, then gently peel away.

Cracking idea

Twinkling candlelight enhances the romance of summer evenings, so have some illumination on hand that bring magic to your outdoor table. If you don't want to bring out your best candleholders, try this original idea using an egg carton and half a dozen eggshells. The shells are filled with candle sand, a material made from tiny beads of wax, which enables you to turn almost any non-flammable receptacle into a candle. Candle sand is sold with a selection of wicks.

1 Break the tops of six eggs and remove the contents, making sure the main part of the shell remains intact. Carefully wash out the shells and leave to dry, then place them in a cardboard egg carton.

2 Carefully fill each shell about half full with candle sand. Insert wicks in the sand and light.

It's a snip

The shapes on this lampshade are simply pieces of paper pasted onto a plain yellow background. The dark areas are created by using a double layer of paper, and here and there you can cut sections out entirely so light shines through.

1 Remove a plain lampshade from its lamp, then locate the seam and position it on a large piece of paper. Mark the paper at the top and bottom of the seam and join the two marks with a straight pencil line. Slowly roll the shade across the paper, drawing along the top and bottom edges as you go, until you come to the seam again. You will end up with the outline of your lampshade drawn on paper.

2 Draw your design on this template, shading areas according to how light or dark you want them. When you're happy with your design, outline the shapes on tracing paper.

3 Transfer the shapes to white and yellow paper. Using sharp scissors or a craft knife, cut them out. Rub off any pencil marks that might show when light shines through.

4 Pour all-purpose white glue into a saucer and, using a brush, apply a thin layer to the backs of the paper shapes. Press them onto the shade, adding extra layers of paper to areas you want to look darker. Let the glue dry thoroughly before cutting sections out with a very sharp craft knife. Apply several coats of clear polyurethane spray varnish, leaving to dry between coats.

TIP
When cutting out sections from the shade, protect your fingers by taping a thick piece of corrugated cardboard inside the shade underneath the area you are cutting.

Hot metal

Create this gorgeous lamp by attaching bands of leaf shapes cut from aluminum foil to a shade made from metal mesh.

1 Make a lampshade template by drawing two semi-circles, 10 1/2 inches apart, on paper. The top edge should measure 22 inches, the bottom 26 3/4 inches. Measure these distances along the arcs and join with a straight line. Cut out the shape. Draw around the template on fine metal mesh and cut out. Join the straight edges with short lengths of fine wire: Double over and poke them through the mesh, then twist the ends together with pliers.

2 Push a 7 3/4-inch-diameter metal ring into base of shade, then attach it to mesh with fine wire. Make a 6 3/4-inch-diameter circle of heavy galvanized wire to fit 1/4 inch below top of shade and wire it into place. Fold over 1/4 inch of mesh at the top.

3 Draw a leaf shape 3 inches high, 2 3/4 inches wide on thin cardboard and cut out. Place on heavy aluminum foil and trace. Repeat to make a band of leaves to fit the shade and cut out with small scissors. Draw veins on backs of leaves with a ballpoint pen. Using a pair of compasses, pierce two holes 1/4 inch from a straight edge between each leaf. Attach the leaves to the shade with fine wire through the holes. Cover shade with more bands. To neaten the top, fold a 1-inch-wide strip of foil over the top edge.

TIP
For safety reasons, it's very important to use this shade only with a lamp-stand and a small light bulb of no more than 40 watts.

All the trimmings

Candy stripes of ribbon in two contrasting colors form a pretty decoration for a plain white lampshade, with braid adding a finishing touch around the top and bottom edges. Pastel colors and flowers would be ideal for a feminine bedroom. There is a wide range of ribbons to choose from, so this idea can very easily be adapted to suit any decor.

1 Measure around the top and bottom rims of your lampshade and lightly pencil eight evenly spaced vertical lines down the shade. Measure the length of the shade and cut pieces of narrow ribbon to size, adding 1 inch (to give a 1/4-inch overlap at the top and a 3/4-inch overlap at the bottom).

2 Put double-sided tape on the back of the ribbon and stick to the shade to cover the pencil lines. Stick the overlaps to the inside of the shade at top and bottom. Measure equal distances between the narrow ribbons and stick lengths of wider contrasting ribbon in place at these points.

3 Cut lengths of braid to fit around the top and bottom rims of the shade, adding 3/4 inch to each length. Secure the braid in place using a glue gun or strong fabric glue, overlapping the ends to give a neat finish.

Cut-price chandelier

If you love the luxurious look of a glittering chandelier but not the price tag, then re-create that sparkle with glass beads dangling from a ring used for a hanging lampshade. You will need a selection of beads in different sizes and shapes: small ones to go around the ring and a mix of long beads and large, round ones for the drops.

1 Decorate a 6-inch-diameter hanging lampshade ring with two coats of enamel paint, then one coat of clear enamel varnish, allowing it to dry between coats. Cut a 27 1/2-inch length of jewelry wire and thread on the first small bead.

Fold over the end of the wire and twist it with small pliers, then continue threading on small beads until there is just 1/4 inch of wire remaining. Fold this over the last bead and twist the wire to secure the beads. Wrap the beaded wire around the ring.

2 To make the bead drops, cut assorted lengths of wire and thread on a selection of glass beads, starting with the heaviest and securing the ends of the wire by twisting it as before. Leave about 1 inch of wire free to secure the drop to the ring.

3 Secure the first bead drop by wrapping the free end of wire tightly around the ring. Repeat this process to make and attach drops evenly, as before. Remove the bulb from the light socket, slip the ring over, then refit the bulb. Do not use the shade with a light bulb of more than 40 watts.

Fringe benefits

Natural materials such as wood and stone are great for adding a touch of warmth and texture to modern rooms decorated in plain, neutral colors. Natural fabrics have the same effect, so try giving a sleek, modern lamp a more laidback look by wrapping the shade in a length of grass matting. A matching fringe conceals the raw edges around the top and bottom and adds further textural interest.

1 Remove the lampshade and measure its height and circumference, adding 3/4 inch to each measurement. Cut a piece of grass matting to this size. Apply fabric glue to both the matting and the shade. Starting at one edge of the matting, roll it onto the shade. Trim away excess matting and make sure the overlap seam is glued securely.

2 To finish, cut lengths of natural fringe to fit around the top and bottom of the shade. Glue in place, positioning as shown in the picture opposite.

TIP
Lampshades can be covered in many different types of fabrics, to suit your style. If you like a more sumptuous look, check out remnant tables for leftover bits of luxurious, expensive materials.

Plastic fantastic

Make a lamp that doubles as a picture and displays your favorite items behind a sheet of laminated plastic. Choose flat objects, such as feathers or leaves, plus a piece of handmade paper as an attractive background. The laminating is done out by pressing the items with an iron between pieces of clear plastic sheeting. Clipping a light bracket behind the plastic turns your picture into an unusual wall lamp.

1 Select the items to be laminated and cut a sheet of handmade paper on which to arrange them. From a roll of plastic sheeting, cut two identical pieces large enough to cover the paper, adding a border of at least 2 1/4 inches all around. Place one plastic sheet on top of some baking parchment, arrange the paper and items on top, and place the other plastic sheet on top, making a sandwich. Cover with another sheet of baking parchment.

2 With a medium-hot iron, carefully press down onto the layers, making sure you cover all the plastic with the heat. You can peek to see if the plastic has bonded. Peel off the baking parchment but take care—it will be hot. Leave to cool.

3 Using a heavy clip, fix a light bracket behind the plastic and mount on the wall to make an unusual lamp. Use it with a light bulb of no more than 40 watts.

Rich glow

Make a lamp base look like a million dollars with a shimmering golden finish. Inexpensive metallic leaf can be applied using traditional gilding techniques, but gives the same glow as real gold for a fraction of the price. To make shopping for the ingredients easy, see if you can find a kit that includes everything you need: metallic gold leaf, size (glue for gilding), shellac and brushes. Choose a lamp base that has a smooth surface.

1 Using a brush, apply a thin layer of size over the entire surface of the lamp base. Leave to dry until the size is tacky to the touch.

2 Carefully lay a sheet of gold leaf onto the tacky surface using a soft brush. Continue applying sheets until the whole base is covered. Don't worry too much if the sheets overlap slightly or if you need to fill in any gaps later, because this will actually enhance the overall effect. Leave to dry, then buff with a soft cloth before sealing with a coat of shellac.

3 Mask off a row of squares all

the way around the lampshade with masking tape. Apply a thin layer of size to each square. Carefully cut the gold leaf to roughly the same dimensions as your masked-off squares, then apply as before. Once the gold leaf is completely dry, remove the masking tape and gently rub away any loose leaf with a soft cloth. Do not seal the shade with shellac.

TIP
Sheets of gilding foil are very fragile and are usually separated by layers of tissue. To avoid damaging the foil, only remove them as you need them and keep the tissue in place until the last second.

Twilight zone

Get your garden glowing on a warm night with soft, diffused light from these stylish lanterns. Fine copper mesh makes a perfect shade for candles and tealights and is easy to fold or bend into shape. Shiny paper fasteners add a cool finishing touch and hold the lantern edges together.

1 Cut a piece of copper mesh to the size required and even up the edges by folding them over twice, as you would to sew a hem. Wrap the mesh around a cylindrical object such as a vase or glass,overlapping the edges, to get the right shape.

2 Using a ruler, measure off marks for the paper fasteners along the overlap, and cut little slits in the mesh at each of these points for the fasteners to slip into. These will keep the lantern in shape. If you like, try pleating the mesh to create a star effect. Place a tealight or candle inside each lantern.

Let it bead

A curtain made from strings of glass beads screens a window pane with droplets of sparkling color as light filters through them. This is a good way to brighten up a dull window without blocking out light.

1 Using a fret saw, cut a length of wooden dowel slightly longer than the width of your window recess. Make pencil marks on the dowel at 2 3/4-inch intervals. Carefully drill a small hole through the dowel at each pencil mark.

2 Arrange beads in rows—the number of rows should equal the number of holes in the dowel. Create a random arrangement of colors and sizes, mixing longer beads with round ones and discs.

3 Cut waxed cotton thread to the length you want your curtain, plus extra for knots between the beads. Tie a knot at one end of the cotton, thread on a bead, then tie a knot on the other side to secure. Thread on the remaining beads in the row, one by one, knotting the cotton before and after each bead and spacing them evenly. For the discs, wind the cotton through the hole and around the bead a couple of times. Repeat with the other rows of beads.

4 Thread the top of each bead string through a hole in the rod, then tie a knot at the top to secure and cut off any excess cotton thread. When you have attached all the bead strings to the rod, flex the dowel and place in the window recess; it will be self-supporting.

TIP
When drilling holes through the dowels, you will find it easier if you secure the rod to your worktop with masking tape or hold it steady using a small clamp. Be careful not to drill through your work surface!

Keep tabs on it

Top tabs give a curtain a contemporary look. Either make a single curtain or, for a wider window, make a pair. You may need to sew two pieces of fabric together to get the width you need.

1 To find the curtain length, measure the depth of your window and add 4 1/2 inches. For the width, measure and add half again, plus 2 1/4 inches. Stitch 1/2-inch double hems on each side edge. Decide how far apart the tabs will be (5 to 6 inches). For each, cut a 10 1/2 × 5 inch fabric strip.

2 Fold each tab in half, right sides facing, and stitch 1/2 inch from edges. Press the seam open with point of iron. Turn each tab to the right side, fold so seam lies in the center and press.

3 Fold each tab to bring raw edges together and pin to top edge of curtain. Space tabs evenly. Cut a fabric strip 4 inches deep and the width of the curtain plus 1 inch. Turn under 1/2 inch on one long edge and stitch. Pin over the tabs, right side down, matching raw edge to curtain edge. Stitch strip to curtain, 1/2 inch from raw edges, then fold away from curtain and press flat. Machine stitch close to seam to hold fabric flat. Fold this piece of fabric to back of curtain and press. Turn under 1/2 inch at each short end and slipstitch to sides of curtain.

4 Hand or machine stitch a double 2-inch hem on lower edge of curtain.

Spot the difference

A café curtain provides privacy during the day by screening the lower half of a window, but you may feel that the traditional gathered or lacy styles look too fussy when teamed with full-length drapes. For a sharper, more contemporary feel, make this neat blind by cutting a series of small circles from silvery foil and sticking them onto clear plastic. A simple sheer curtain softens the look slightly and can be drawn across to give greater privacy at night.

1 Cut a panel of clear plastic to size. Cut circles from aluminum foil using small sharp scissors. To get perfect circles, draw around an object such as a can or bottle. Glue the circles onto the plastic in evenly spaced rows.

2 To hang the blind, make holes along the top edge using a hole punch and insert small split rings. Thread a length of fine wire through the rings and fix it to hooks at either side of the window frame.

Rising sun

Based on a Japanese door panel, this design works just as well on a window. Dip-dyeing creates a graduated effect on the panels of the curtain.

1 For the top panel, cut a strip of cotton fabric 3/4 inch wider than the window and about a third of the depth. For the lower panels, cut one piece to cover the rest of the window, adding 2 1/4 inches to both length and width. Wash these pieces and some leftover fabric (to use for tabs). Leave damp.

2 Mark three equally spaced points along the top panel, pinch the points between your fingers and wrap tightly with string. Mix cold water dye according to instructions, then immerse the string-tied strip and tab fabric in the dye bath. Rinse, untie string, dry and press.

3 To dye the remaining fabric, pin with clothespins to a rod placed across two chairs. Immerse lower half into dye bath, then raise 12 inches or so every 20 minutes. Rinse, dry and press, then cut into three equal panels. Stitch a 1/4-inch hem on sides and base of each panel, and on side edges of top panel. Join lower panels to bottom edge of top panel and trim seam to neaten.

4 For tabs, cut 2 × 6 3/4 inch strips, press 1/4 inch to wrong side on both long edges of each, then fold in half lengthwise with pressed edges inside and stitch close to edges. Follow step 3 on page 188 to finish.

TIP
Keep the Japanese theme going by hanging the curtain from a bamboo pole. Support it using center brackets, then decorate the pole ends with tassels.

Chain gang

This super-cool modern shade runs smoothly on silvery chains. Choose a sheer fabric and buy fine nickel-plated chain five times the length of your window. Eyelets are available in a kit that includes the hole punch.

1 Cut fabric to the size of your window, adding 1 1/2 inches to width, 4 inches to length. Make a 1/4-inch double hem on each side edge, and a 1-inch double hem on bottom edge. Starting just above bottom hem, mark eyelet positions 4 inches from side edges and 8 inches apart. Fix eyelets following kit instructions.

2 Cut a 10-inch square batten to width of shade and drill a hole at each end. On underside of batten, fix one screw eye 4 inches from each end and a third 3/4 inch from end of the cleat (double hook). Using a staple gun, fix top edge of shade to top of batten, doubling fabric over for strength. Insert a 2-inch steel rod through bottom hem and sew hem ends closed.

3 Starting at opposite side from cleat, and working from front of blind, thread the chain up through all the screw eyes on the batten. Allow enough chain to hang down on the cleat side of the shade as far as the cleat position, then double it back on itself, thread it through the two nearest screw eyes and down through remaining eyelets.

4 Fix a washer to each chain end, using pliers to pry open the links. Fix batten in place by screwing through holes into window frame. Fix cleat at hand height on the frame.

TIP

If you can't be bothered with sewing, use iron-on tape for the hems and you won't even have to pick up a needle.

On the wire

Make fun shapes from fine copper wire, then display them in see-through pockets stitched to a curtain panel. Choose sheer fabrics for both curtain and pockets, so that the light shines through to show off the shapes. Use copper tubing as a pole, adding decorative finials at both ends of the pole.

1 Cut fabric to the size of your window, adding 2 1.2 inches to the length and 3/4 inch to the width. Stitch a 1/4-inch hem on each side edge, and a 1-inch double hem along the bottom edge of the fabric. To make and attach the tabs, cut 6 3/4-inch squares of fabric, then follow instructions for steps 2 and 3 of the tab-top curtain on page 188.

2 To make the colored pockets, cut rectangles from contrasting fabrics. Fray the edges, then pin the pockets at random to the curtain. Using contrasting

embroidery thread, sew small running stitches 1/2 inch from the side and bottom edges of each pocket.

3 Use pliers to bend 1/4-inch

copper wire into simple shapes to fit into the pockets—spirals, daisies and leaves are all easy. Attach 7 1/2-inch center brackets to the window frame. Slot a copper tube through the tabs and brackets, and then twirl copper wire around the tube ends to make finials. Slot a wire shape into each of the pockets.

Frosty outlook

If you want to screen a small window without sewing a stitch, take a look at the array of beautiful handmade papers available from stationery stores, art supply stores and craft shops. With designs and textures to equal the finest fabrics, they can be glued onto lengths of bamboo to make a simple blind. To make the most of the light, choose thin papers in pale colors—the delicate texture and fern design of this one gives the look of a frosted window pane.

1 Screw a cup hook into each side of your window frame. Cut a piece of bamboo long enough to extend slightly past the hooks.

2 Trim handmade paper to fit the window, adding 2 inches to the length. Use double-sided tape to stick the paper to the pole, making sure it is centered and hanging straight. Cut more bamboo to the width of the paper and, using the tape, stick it to the base of the blind to weigh it down.

Instant solutions

Tablecloths, napkins and even kitchen towels or sheets can all make excellent quick-fix window treatments. As they are already hemmed, there is no sewing required, and if you use clips to hang them you don't need to worry about any hardware, either. The top of a tablecloth can be folded over to adjust it to the right length and make a decorative valance. Kitchen towels and napkins are the perfect size for making café curtain panels—simply position your pole according to their size so that they hang to meet the sill at the bottom.

1 To make a curtain, take a heavy linen tablecloth of the right size to cover your window: For fullness it should be at least one-and-a-half times the width of the window. If you want a decorative valance, the cloth should be 8 to 12 inches longer than the length of the window. Fold over the valance at the top, adjusting its depth so that the curtain hangs at the right length, and iron.

2 Fix curtain clips along the fold, spacing them equally. To hang the curtain, simply hook the clips onto the rings of a curtain pole.

Individual style

If you've got a plain window shade that needs to be livened up, an easy and very effective way to customize it is by inserting a decorative mat or table runner in the center. Choose a mat with a design that complements the color of your shade, so that the insert blends in well with its surroundings. If you prefer, you could use several smaller table mats or napkins rather than one large one, dotting them around at random over the shade.

1 Lay a plain window shade out on a flat surface. Place a decorative mat in the center so that it will be well-positioned when the shade is down. Pin the mat in place, then machine or hand sew close to its edges.

2 Carefully cut away the shade behind the mat, about 1/4 inch away from the stitching.

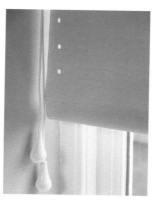

TIP
For an even simpler way of customizing a brightly colored window shade, try punching a row of holes down the sides.

Mirror magic

A plain curtain gets a retro look with oblong patches of felt that act as windows for small mirrors. This adds a reflective twinkle to your drapes as the mirrors catch the light. A glazier should be able to cut the pieces of mirror to size for you. Choose felt in a selection of different colors that harmonize with your curtain fabric.

1 Get leftover mirror pieces cut to the size you want. From thin cardboard, cut an oblong template 1/4 inch larger all around than the mirrors, then use it to cut shapes from colored felt.

2 Cut oval windows from the felt patches, then use matching embroidery thread to sew a running stitch around the cut window edge, to prevent any stretching.

3 Stitch the felt patches at random to your curtain, sewing with embroidery thread and running stitch around their outer edges. Slip a mirror into each felt window before sewing the top edge closed.

Head start

The ruffled top on these elegant curtains is created using heading tape. Cords woven into it pull up to form pleats or gathers.

1 The tape instructions will explain how wide the fabric must be to allow for gathering. Cut fabric to required size, adding 8 inches to the length for hems and heading. Make double 1/2-inch hems down each side. Hem bottom edge by turning up 3/4 inch then 2 inches.

2 On top edge of curtain, iron 4 inches to wrong side and tack close to raw edge. Cut heading tape to width of curtain, plus 1 1/2 inches. Position tape right side up and 3 inches down from top edge so it hides raw heading edge and extends 3/4 inch beyond each side. Pin in place. At leading edge of curtain, pull tape cords from wrong side of tape and knot together. Turn under 3/4 inch of raw end of tape and pin.

3 On remaining end of heading tape, pull out cords and leave free. Tuck in 3/4 of raw end of tape. Stitch heading tape in place along top and lower edges, working in the same direction each time to stop any puckering.

4 Pull up loose cord ends to gather curtain to half the window's width. Loosely knot cord ends to secure. Make sure gathers are even, then insert hooks into pockets in the tape, spacing them 4 inches apart. Wind loose cord into a bundle and secure with a few stitches. Don't cut off the excess.

TIP

Sew velvet ribbon along the top and leading edges of your curtains to add a graceful finishing touch.

Spring blooms

Give a window a fresh look for spring by making a simple, sheer white panel scattered with pretty blue flowers. The blooms are fixed to the fabric using an iron-on bonding material, which offers a quick no-sew method of fusing one fabric to another.

1 Cut a piece of sheer fabric, such as linen voile, to the size of your window, adding 1 1/2 inches to the width and 5 1/2 inches to the length for hems. Make 1/4-inch double hems down the side edges. Turn up 3/4 inch then 2 inches along the top and bottom edges, then machine stitch.

2 To make the flowers, take a fabric in a contrasting color.

Following the manufacturer's instructions, lay the iron-on bonding material on the wrong side of this fabric and iron on. Draw a flower design on cardboard and cut it out to make a template. Using this, draw flower shapes on the backing of the bonding material, then cut out.

3 Lay the voile on a flat surface and arrange the flower shapes on top. When they are positioned the way you want, remove the bonding backing. Cover the shapes with a damp cloth and press to secure them.

4 To hang the panel, place clips and rings along its top edge and thread the rings onto a pole.

WHERE TO BUY:

ARTS AND CRAFTS AND DECORATIVE EFFECTS

BJ'S CRAFT SUPPLIES
Specializes in beads, ribbons, raffia and all types of craft kits. New items are added regularly.
www.bjcraftsupplies.com
Tel: 362 286 3719

DESIGNER STENCILS
Stencils in numerous designs and shpes for all sized needs.
Tel: 800 822 STEN

DICK BLICK ART MATERIALS
Dick Blick Art Materials has been mailing its famous art supplies catalog since 1911. You'll find a wide variety of brushes, ceramics, mosaics, crafts and cutting tools here.
Tel: 800 828 4548
www.dickblick.com

ETCHWORLD
Supplies for the etching, painting and engraving of glass.
Tel: 800 872 3485
www.etchworld.com

FACTORY DIRECT CRAFT SUPPLY
This outlet supplier has thousands of crafts supplies arranged alphabetically from adhesives and angels to musical buttons to soapmaking, wire, wood and wreaths.
Tel: 800 252 5223
www.factorydirect.com

FAUX STORE
Faux finishes, custom imprints and more.
Tel: 800 270 8871
www.fauxstore.com

FISCHER AND JIROUCH
Hand carved molding and mantels in many styles.
Tel: 216 361 0650
www.fischerandjirouch.com

GODDESS DESIGNS
Stamps, stencils and art supplies in a huge range of designs.
www.goddessdesigns.com

JEWELRY SUPPLY.COM

Beads are the specialty here—glass, silver, crystal, stone, and anything else you can think of.
Tel: 916 780 9610
www.jewelrysupply.com

PEARL FINE ART SUPPLIES

The online branch of New York City's giant art supplier, Pearl Paint, has everything from handcrafted papers to golf leaf to craft kits, pens, and, of course, paints—in thousands of types and colors. Everything is high-quality and discount priced.
www.pearlpaint.com

PLAID

Supplies for fabric painting, stenciling, mosaic tiling and more.
Tel: 800 842 4197
www.plaid.com

SUNSHINE DISCOUNT CRAFTS

This outlet has been around since 1980 and has a huge selection for serious crafters. A good place for foam, fluff and similar items that may be hard to find elsewhere.
www.sunshinecrafts.com

TBJS CRAFT SUPPLIES

Beads, chimes, craft kits and general art supplies.
Tel: 361 286 3719
www.bjscraftsupplies.com

WHITE RIVER ORNAMENTALS

Moldings, mantles and other handcarved pieces for the home.
Tel: 800 558 0119
www.mouldings.com

FABRICS AND WALLPAPERS

ABLONDER HOME ACCENTS
Wallpaper for for every decor in many shades and fabrics.
Tel: 800 321 4070
www.blonderwall.com

BREWSTER WALLCOVERING COMPANY
They carry a wide selection of contemporary wallcoverings, borders and fabrics.
Tel: 800 366 1700
www.brewsterwallcovering.com

EISENHART WALLCOVERINGS
A wide range of wallcoverings and fabrics from playful for the kids to elegant for you.
Tel: 800 931 WALL
www.eisenhartwallcoverings.com

HOME DEPOT
A major retail outlet for all your home improvement needs, they carry many different brands and patterns of wallcoverings.
Tel: 800 430 3376
www.homedepot.com

F SCHUMACHER & CO.
A wide selection of wallpapers, rugs and fabrics for every decor and every room.
www.fschumacher.com

IMPERIAL HOME DECOR GROUP
Wallpaper and borders in many different styles for every room.
Tel: 888 608 5943
www.ihdg.com

INTERIOR MALL
This is an online source for all you intrior decorating needs. Order online on by telephone.
Tel: 800 590 5884
www.interiormall.com

LAURA ASHLEY
Classic and country-style fabrics and papers, especially florals.
Tel: 800 463 8075
www.laura-ashleyusa.com

PLAID
Supplies for fabric painting, stenciling, mosaic tiling and more.
Tel: 800 842 4197
www.plaid.com

RAG SHOP
Fabrics and arificial flowers to spruce up the home.
Tel: 973 423 1303
www.ragshop.com

SEABROOK
A vast array of floral and country patterns to pretty up your home.
Tel: 800 238 9152
www.seabrookwallcoverings.com

SHERWIN WILLIAMS
Well-known for their paint, check out their collection of wallpaper and borders.
www.sherwinwilliams.com

VILLAGE HOME
Wallpaper and borders in many materials including fabrics and vinyls.
www.villagehome.com

PAINTS, VARNISHES AND SPECIAL FINISHES

ACE HARDWARE
Paint and paint supplies including stencils and painting advice.
Tel: 630 990 6600
www.acehardware.com

BENJAMIN MOORE
A wide selection of indoor and outdoor paints and stains in many colors and finishes.
Tel: 800 344 0400
www.benjaminmoore.com

BIOSHIELD
Solvent free and water based house paint for a heathier household. Many colors and finishes available.
Tel: 800 621 2591
www.ecopaint.com

DUTCH BOY
Well-known for their interior and exterior paint, this company offers a wide variety of colors and finishes.
Tel: 800 828 5669
www.dutchboy.com

FULLER O'BRIEN
Quality paint with affordable prices in a wide selection of colors and finishes.
www.fullerpaint.com

GLIDDEN
Well-known for their paint, this company offers a wide variety of colors and finishes.
Tel: 800 GLIDDEN
www.gliddenpaint.com

HOME DEPOT

Major retail outlet for all your
home improvement needs,
they carry many designer
paint brands as well as lower
priced ones.
Tel: 800 430 3376
www.homedepot.com

SHERWIN WILLIAMS

Popular paint store carries
many brands, finishes and
colors, including the Martha
Stewart line.
www.sherwinwilliams.com

UNFINISHED FURNITURE

FURNITURE SHOPPING TIPS

This web site offers links to a variety of companies that sell unfinished furniture—some locally and some nationwide. Also includes suggestions for the best places on the web to find used furniture.
www.furnitureshoppingtips.com/unfinishedfurniture.html

POP'S UNFINISHED FURNITURE

An online store offering unfinished furniture of all types, from dressers to tables and chests, bookcases and also small accessories. The site includes helpful articles about what to look for when you're buying unfinished furniture. Clearance sales offers some real bargains.
Tel: 888 838 0707
www.popsfurniture.com

UNFINISHED FURNITURE ASSOCIATION

Although there is a lot of association news on the web site of this business organization, they also provide lists of retailers, suppliers and manufacturers of unfinished furniture that are very helpful.
Tel: 800 487 8321
www.unfiishedfurniture.org

ACE HARDWARE
Helpful advice for painting, installations, working with tools, lighting and toerh electrical equiptment.
Tel: 630 990 6600
www.acehardware.com

BENJAMIN MOORE
Helpful tips for painting and getting the decorative effects you want.
Tel: 800 344 0400
www.benjaminmoore.com

BETTER HOMES AND GARDENS
Advice on decorating and arranging all the rooms in the house from the magazine experts.
www.bhg.com

CONSUMER REPORTS
Reports on all major appliances and nearly all brand name products, including mattresses.
www.consumerreports.org

HOME DEPOT
Helpful tips fpr paintings, putting in bathroom fixtures and lighting and more.
Tel: 800 430 3376
www.homedepot.com

HOME FURNISH.COM
Advice on picking out bed-room furniture and mattresses, as well as finding the right sized mattress for your room.
www.homefurnish.com

STENCIL ARTISANS LEAGUE, INC.
Helpful stencil tips, where to find the best designs and more.
Tel: 505 865 9119
www.sali.com

CONTRIBUTORS

BBC Worldwide and *BBC Good Homes* magazine would like to thank the following contributors.

Jo Barnes: page 154
Juliet Bawden: pages 42, 56, 62, 64, 82, 158, 174, 186
Evelyn Bennett: page 162
Petra Boase: pages 76, 106, 176
Chloe Brown: pages 30, 128
Jane Burdon: pages 26
Jo Carmichael: page 86
Sacha Cohen: pages 122, 124, 126
Jan Dabbous: pages 66, 68, 70, 72, 146, 202
Alison Davidson: page 144
Cris Donet: page 110
Marion Elliott: pages138, 172, 190
Mary Fitzmaurice: pages 192, 194, 196

Jane Forster: page 100
Mark Gregory: page 54
Emma Hardy: page 208
Zoe Hope: pages 32, 84
Alison Jenkins: pages 24, 104, 114, 152, 182, 204
Jayne Keeley: page 164
Tracey Kendall: page134
Andrea Maflin: page 96
Lucyina Moodie: page 78
Neeley Moore: pages 40, 80
Kitty Percy: pages 8, 10, 12, 14, 20, 22, 88, 130, 136, 166, 168, 170
Nicky Phillips: page 18
Maggie Philo: pages 46, 160
Sophie Robinson: pages148, 178, 200
Fran Soler: page 142
Wendy Uren: pages 28, 108, 206
Lynda Watts: pages 36, 52, 102
Wendy Wilson: pages 48, 132